What Was Taken, What Remains

Isla Rue

Published by Tree Of Life Publishing, 2025.

WHAT WAS TAKEN, WHAT REMAINS

First edition. June 3, 2025.

Copyright © 2025 Isla Rue.

ISBN: 979-8231672240

Written by Isla Rue.

Table of Contents

What Was Taken, What Remains
by Isla Rue

Dedication

To my daughters—Renata, Brielle, Zara, and Renee.

You are my why. My reason. My breath.

To my grandchildren—may your lives be filled with wonder, your hearts shielded from harm, and your spirits always free.

To my husband, James—thank you for walking beside me, especially when the road was uneven.

To my friend Solace—thank you for listening without judgment and for helping me remember that every story deserves to be told.

To my mom, thank you.

Letter to My Daughters and Grandchildren

If you're reading this, it means I found the courage to put it all into words.

This isn't just my story—it's part of yours too.

Every chapter I lived shaped the way I loved you.

I made mistakes. I carried pain. I broke, and I healed, and broke again.

But through it all, I never stopped trying.

I want you to know that cycles can be broken.

That truth can be spoken.

That love, even when wounded, can still be whole.

I wrote this so you'll never forget where you come from,

And so you'll always know where you're free to go.

With all my love,

Mom / Grandma

Chapter One: The Cold Beach

It was cold that morning—oddly cold for the beach. In my young mind, the ocean had always belonged to warmth, sun, and laughter. But that day, I shivered in my blue shorts and sleeveless white blouse. My favorite white sandals were already filled with soft grains of sand, clinging to my toes like secrets.

I couldn't have been more than three years old. Yet the memory is clear—etched like sea glass: smoothed by time, but never gone. I can still hear the waves, smell the salt air, and feel the thrill of being alone with my dad.

This was my day. My sister wasn't allowed to come. Just me and Daddy. I imagine I was smiling so big it hurt, my tiny hand wrapped tightly around his fingers as we walked the shore.

He had brought me to check on the boat—and to spend time together. I felt like a princess, chosen and cherished. One-on-one time with him was rare. It couldn't get any better.

I kept looking up at him, full of love and the kind of trust only a child can give. He was tall—six foot two—and strong, at least from where I stood. Gorgeous brown hair, piercing green eyes. My protector. My hero. My dad.

I used to shrug my shoulders up and down when I was happy. That morning, I remember doing it a lot.

We had breakfast at a restaurant right on the beach. It was early, and the sky was painted in shades of pink and orange—like magic spilling across the horizon. Everything about the morning felt perfect.

He ordered one of everything on the menu—literally. The table overflowed. I had never seen so much food in my life. At home with my mom and grandparents, money was tight. There was always enough, but never more than that. This? This was something else.

My dad didn't eat—just drank coffee and watched me with a smile. I'd finish one plate, and he'd slide another over. "Here, try this," he'd say. I took at least a nibble of everything.
I hope I never forget how happy that little girl felt. I wish the memory stopped there—on that magical morning, with a full belly and my daddy beside me.
But it didn't.
If I could rewrite that day, I'd end it differently. He would scoop me up, toss me over his shoulder with my legs around his neck. We'd laugh,
twirling down the shoreline, joy echoing over the waves. He'd be happy. I'd be safe.
But that's not how it went.
After breakfast, we headed to the boat. My stomach was too full. I didn't yet know what that would mean on choppy water. The beach was empty, like we were the only people in the world. The ocean looked restless.
The boat was small—a motorboat with a couple of seats and a cooler near where I sat. I didn't ask what was in it. I didn't think to.
He buckled himself into a life vest.
Said there wasn't one in my size, and that I wouldn't need it.
They say I was articulate for my age. I probably chattered through breakfast, but on the boat, I was quiet. Something in me shifted. I felt uneasy.
The boat started slowly. The smell of salt filled my nose, and cold mist kissed my skin. I looked down at my sandals and saw how the sand had changed—no longer soft and warm, but damp, clumpy, dark. It had followed me from the shore, hitching a ride into the boat. Funny, the things you remember.
When I looked up again, we were far
from land. The buildings behind us looked tiny. The world had gotten bigger—and we were alone in it.

He stopped the motor and stood, gazing out at the sea. The water was choppy, and the boat rocked gently. I wasn't enjoying it. My stomach twisted.

Then he walked over, picked me up, and held me close. Maybe I'd said something earlier, but I don't remember. What I do remember are his words:

"You really need to learn how to swim. Your sister knows how. Wouldn't you like to know too?"

I watched his mouth move as he spoke, my arms around his neck. "Yes, Daddy," I said eagerly. Of course I wanted to learn. I didn't understand he meant now. I didn't know how cold the water would be.

The next moment was chaos. I was underwater—reaching for something, anything—but finding nothing. My eyes burned. My throat burned. The silhouette of my dad blurred above me. The boat drifted away. My sandals felt like anchors.

Somehow, I kicked hard enough to break the surface. "Daddy!" I screamed. I saw him—for a moment— standing there. Then he was gone again. I sank.

I heard the motor start. He's trying to find me! I have to get up! I clawed my way back to the surface—but the boat had vanished. Maybe he fell in too? Panic swallowed me.

Something wrapped around my foot—seaweed. But I didn't know what that was. I thought it was a monster, an ocean creature trying to eat me. Terror gave me strength. I fought.

When I finally rose again, I saw the boat. My dad hadn't fallen. He was looking for me.

I don't know how, but I reached the boat. I was able to scream, "Daddy, I want out! Daddy, I can't!" But I was so tired. So weak. I began to shut down.

Still, I think he really wanted me to learn to swim. I went under again.
I couldn't fight anymore. My body gave in. I felt the water fill my
throat. And as I drifted, I thought: Poor Daddy. I should've learned to
swim.
Then—arms. I was being lifted. Back in the boat. My dad was holding
me, crying, repeating, "I'm so sorry, I'm sorry, I'm sorry." I was
shaking, teeth chattering.
He opened the cooler—and somehow,
like magic, there was a lifejacket my size. And a blanket. He put the
vest on me, wrapped me up. I kept whispering, "I'm sorry, Daddy. I'm
sorry."
He didn't respond. He just stared at me, tears falling.
I looked down. Something green still clung to my sandals—the
seaweed. My dad unbuckled them. And I was safe.
He pulled me next to him and restarted the motor. We headed back to
shore. I don't remember if he said anything else. I only remember
throwing up all over the boat. The sky had changed again. It was colder
now.

That was the day my dad tried to kill me.
It was also the day he realized he couldn't.
Somewhere deep inside, something in me changed. The part that tries
to do everything right. The part that takes the blame. Even now,
knowing what I know, I still feel the shame.
I still feel sorry, for him.

—-

Chapter 2: Scrubbed Away

Life is filled with memories—some good, some bad. As I tell my story, I'll do my best to fill in the gaps. Some pieces are crystal clear. Others feel more like echoes.

When my dad brought me back to my grandparents' house, I remember the look on their faces—surprise, maybe even fear. Or maybe that's just the emotion I've layered onto the memory over time. Sometimes I wonder... did they know the plan all along?

My grandpa rushed toward me and scooped me up in his arms. He loved me. I loved him. He was my safe place in a world that rarely felt safe.

We weren't well off. We lived in the back of the thrift store they ran—selling used clothes and forgotten things people no longer needed. Sometimes my sister and I would play dress-up in the store, putting on silly shows for them.

We had no television, just a radio. No indoor plumbing—only an outhouse out back. There was never any toilet paper. We used catalog pages from Sears or JCPenney. Maybe that's why, to this day, I refuse to buy one-ply. I think I've earned my Charmin.

Baths were a treat. We'd heat water in a giant pot on the stove and pour it into a metal basin placed on the kitchen's dirt floor. A curtain hung in the doorway—that was our privacy. Most of the time, though, we bathed outside.

The outdoor shower was nothing more than a hose, a wooden pallet to stand on, and rules: you kept your undergarments on.

But not this time.

After my "swimming lesson," I was filthy,and exhausted. I mean, who wouldn't be after swimming for their life?

My grandmother, Cressida, took me outside to clean me up. This time, I was stripped completely naked. Maybe I was that dirty. Maybe she needed me to feel that exposed.

The hose water poured over me as I stood barefoot on the pallet. It was warm compared to the icy ocean. Maybe two degrees warmerbut it felt like a luxury.

Then I saw the corn husk. We used it sometimes to scrub ourselves clean. I reached for it, but she slapped my hand away.

"No," she said. "I'm washing you today."

She grabbed my arm, the dry husk in her other hand. It was brittle and rough.

"Ow!" I cried without thinking.

She stooped down until we were nose to nose, eyes locked.

"I don't want to hear another sound out of you," she hissed. "I'm going to rub all this black off of you if it's the last thing I do."

Sometimes, I wish it had been the last thing she did.

She scrubbed. Hard. My skin peeled in patches. The salt from the ocean still clung to me, and the raw spots burned. I cried. Until she saw me crying. Then she raised her hand like she might hit me.

So I stopped crying.

I couldn't stop wincing, though. That pain is burned into me—more permanent than any scar.

When she was done, I looked like a burn victim. My arms stung so badly I couldn't let them rest at my sides. Naked, stiff, I shuffled into the house like a little Frankenstein.

My grandfather looked at me—then quickly looked away. Cressida followed close behind, pressing her hand into my back, right between my shoulder blades.

"Walk. Walk. I don't have all day."

I tried to walk faster, but I was confused. I was hurting. I wanted my mom, but I hadn't seen her in months. Somewhere deep in my small heart, I already knew there would be no comfort for me.

My sister sat on the bed in the room we shared. Cressida barked at her to find something for me to wear.

"What happened?" my sister asked, her baby voice full of concern.

I turned to Cressida for the answer. She stood with her hands on her hips. "Go ahead. Tell her what happened."

But I didn't know how. I didn't have the words—and even if I did, I wasn't sure I was allowed to speak them.

So I turned back to my sister and said the only thing I could: "Nothing."

That day taught me a lesson I still struggle with:
Say what they need you to say,
or suffer the consequences.

Chapter 3: I'm Okay

The majority of my youth was a mix of confusion. The day of the boat ride was the beginning of the change in who I was meant to be, to who I ultimately became. Nature versus nurture if you will. If this was where all the dysfunction ended, I think I may have emotionally survived.

Life went on, and the day that lasted an eternity was never discussed. My physical wounds healed. To my surprise and relief, and my grandmothers dismay. She could not scrub the black off of me.

Was there remorse from her? Absolutely not. Did my grandfather ask if I was alright? Not even once. Life just continued, without skipping a beat.

Wearing clothes hurt for a bit. But, if I grimaced at any time, I soon followed up with a smile. I'm okay, I'm always okay. Even when I'm not, I'm okay.

It had been month's since I had seen my mom. We didn't have phones, so my sister and I had no communication with her during this time. In a weird way, the thought of her finding out what happened kept me going. "Wait till I tell mommy what happened!" Although, I still really didn't know what happened.

You would think that my grandmother would have been extra nice to me, seeing that my mom was coming home. In hopes that maybe she could convince me not to say anything. However,she wasn't.

The weeks that followed "The Scouring," were filled with insults and blaming. I was told that I was the reason my mom would not have the life she deserved. I was to blame for EVERYONE not having the life and things they could have. My very existence had brought such undo hardship on EVERYONE I loved. I was only three,but I remember everything that was said to me. Why? Why do I remember so much? Cressida would have my sister sit between her legs and brush her hair every morning. I would sit with my back against the wall waiting on my turn. Cressida would say things like,"Look at this beautiful hair, you're never gonna have hair like this."

When it was my turn,she was never as gentle. She would tighten her legs around me and yank my hair as if she couldn't take the time to work the tangles out. So, she would just pull the brush through until the brush freed itself. I never made a sound. By the time I was done, there were little piles of hair clumps on the floor from the tangles that were literally pulled out. "Your hair is unruly!" Is what she said,"Nothing like your sister's. Your sister has white people's hair. I don't know what kind of hair you have!" "Sorry Cressida." Is all I would say. I always apologized.

The Reunion

Today is the day my mom would be home and I will be safe! Do I remember having that thought? No, but I am sure that the excitement was there.

I heard a car pull up and I knew it was my mom! My sister and I ran through the shop, and out the door to greet her! She looked so beautiful as I remember. She smelled of perfume and her clothes looked new! My mommy! Now Cressida would get what's coming! As I hugged my mom, I began to cry. I didn't have to hide it anymore! I guess she could feel me shaking. She gently peeled me off of her and said,"Isla, you're going to dirty my new clothes!" I looked up at her and she nudged me aside to greet her parent's.

I stood there as she walked towards them. There was excitement and laughter. The taxi driver and I were the only ones left outside as the rest of the family went inside.

The driver unloaded my mom's luggage and left them at the shop door. I stood next to them and could see everyone talking inside.

My mom hurried towards me. She grabbed two of the suitcases and kept talking to my grandparents and sister. "Wait until you see what I brought everybody!"

I finally made my way in and sat on the floor beside my sister. I couldn't get over how beautiful my mom was.

Chapter Four: She Was Born

"Some wounds don't bleed. They whisper. And the whisper becomes
your name."
My mother's return home wasn't what I had imagined. She never
asked why I'd been crying, and I never brought it up. I never told her
what Cressida had done. The only thing I mentioned was nearly
drowning.
Her reaction? Dismissive.
"You're being dramatic," she said.
Was I?

She didn't sit my sister and me down to explain where she had been.
Maybe she thought we were too young. Maybe she didn't think we'd
understand. But when she told our grandparents about her trip, we
were all ears. That is, until we lost interest. Still, one thing stuck, she
had been to the States.
The States! That sounded magical. And it wasn't even her first time.
She was so lucky.
"Southport is just gorgeous," she gushed more than once.
"Lisette's house is just magnificent." Lisette was her older sister, our
aunt.
I caught bits and pieces of her stories here and there. Honestly, they
didn't sound that interesting to me, but I listened anyway, hoping to
hear something, anything magical. One morning, I crouched near the
door to listen more closely.
Well, it wasn't a real door. Just a heavy piece of wood rigged into place.
That's when Cressida found me.

She shoved the door open and yanked me up like I weighed nothing. She stood me upright, gripping my arms so tightly I could feel her rage vibrating through me.

"You don't need to be listening to grown-up conversations!" she shouted.

She dragged me across the room and threw me onto the bed like I was trash. Then she grabbed my left ear and twisted it so hard I thought it might tear clean off.

"You know what you use these for? No, you don't. Because you don't use them for anything good. You're a no-good little bitch."

Her slap landed squarely across the left side of my face. My head snapped sideways. My skin burned. My ears rang.

I cried this time. How could I not?

I curled into a tight ball on the bed, sobbing, my body trembling uncontrollably.

"That's what you're good for," Cressida said coldly. "Piece of shit."

Minutes passed. Then my mother walked in.

She wasn't frantic, just cautious. Maybe a little annoyed.

"What happened?" she asked, scanning the room before landing on Cressida.

"What did she do?" she added, gesturing toward me.

She didn't comfort me. Didn't sit beside me or reach for my hand. Not until she knew if I had deserved it. Cressida didn't blink.

"She was born," she said.

That was it.

My mother leaned over and picked me up. I clung to her like a lifeline. My cheek stung. My ear throbbed. And the buzzing in my head didn't stop for days.

Chapter Five: The Last Kiss

"She kissed my head and said she'd be right back. But some kisses carry more silence than promise—and some goodbyes never echo loud enough to prepare you."

The life I had wasn't all bad. I'm sure of it.

There were moments—bright, happy moments—that felt whole and warm. But somehow, they got swallowed up. The dysfunction, the chaos, the trauma—they grew like a cancer, crowding out the good. Leaving no room for joy to settle in and take root as a memory.

One day, my mom told me we were going on a little trip. She had already packed most of my things. My sister was staying behind, but that didn't worry me. I wasn't afraid to be with my mom. Not at all. I wasn't uncomfortable or hesitant. In fact, I was thrilled. I was finally away from Cressida.

Maybe my mom knew all along how I'd been treated. Maybe she was rescuing me. Maybe we were starting over—just the two of us. This felt like a good day.

We didn't stop much on the journey. She had packed sandwiches, drinks, and snacks for the road. We boarded a bus—not quite a Greyhound, but similar. Dirtier. Hotter. No air conditioning. Still, I didn't mind.

We rode for what felt like forever. At least one night, maybe two, we slept on the bus. I curled up beside her, the two of us sharing a large shawl when the air turned cool. I remember feeling safe. I remember that warmth.

Eventually, the bus pulled into a busy, bustling city—San Viero.

I had never left Soltera before, and this place—this city—was alive in a way I had never seen. We didn't do much sightseeing, but we stopped for a hot meal. We were both exhausted. We'd walked nearly two miles with our bags, and my little legs ached. I sat at a table, finishing lunch, while my mom stood, leaned down, and kissed the top of my head.

"I'll be right back," she said.

And then she was gone.

That was the last time I saw my mother for the next three and a half years.

I stayed in my seat like I was told. But as the minutes stretched, fear crept in. Where did she go? Was she lost? This was a new city, after all.

I stuffed my mouth with food, hoping to quiet the sobs rising in my throat. I didn't want to cry out loud. I didn't want anyone to notice I was alone.

And then someone did.

A man approached the table. He looked like Santa Claus—only darker.

"Hello, little one," he said gently. "Your mommy wants you to come with me."

I looked up at him, eyes full of tears, cheeks full of food. I tried to smile. He gathered the bags. All of them were mine. Only mine.

I was the only one getting a new home.

That day, I learned something I'll never forget:

Nothing is ever quite what it seems.

And happiness is always short-lived.

—-

Chapter Six: The Rules

There are parts of my life that feel blocked out. Not forgotten—just buried. I was only two or three, and already I had experienced more than most adults ever will.

I've never told anyone about this. Not really. And honestly, it's not the kind of story you bring up at family functions. There's never a good time to say it out loud.

I won't detail the day-to-day moments of the next three, maybe three and a half years. They don't matter. Not really. As far as I'm concerned, there were no good moments. Not one.

I didn't know why I was with that man. I didn't understand the situation—I just knew I had no say in it. No choice.

Here's what I do remember:

We drove for a long time. I sat up front with him, staring out the window, trying to understand where I was going—or why. He kept saying I was cute. That everything would be fine. Then, like it was the most natural thing in the world, he began listing the rules.

The rules were simple:

1. Don't make unnecessary noise.
2. Never speak unless spoken to.
3. Don't go into the refrigerator without permission.
4. If he asks you to do something, do it. Don't ask why.
5. Don't ask about your family. He is your family.
6. If you go anywhere with him, say he's your dad.
7. Call him Daddy—always.
8. He can add more rules anytime he wants.

I doubt he said them exactly like that—he probably simplified them for a toddler. But the message was clear: Obey. Smile. Pretend.

When we finally got to his house, it was dark. Isolated. He had a
dog—I remember that. It wandered in and out like it owned the place.
The house was gloomy. Heavy curtains. Dark furniture. The floor
wasn't dirt—that felt like a good thing. I'd been to his house before,
but only to visit. Now it was home.
He brought in the bags and sat on the sofa.
"Come here," he said.
I froze.
I didn't know him. I didn't want to go near him.
When was my mom coming?

He called again. Still no name—just, "Hey, come here."
I didn't move.
Then I heard his footsteps. Heavy. Closer.
"You didn't hear me?" he asked. I nodded.
"I'll forgive you this time," he said. "But next time I call you, you better
come."
He picked me up and set me on his lap. Played with my hair. I was
shaking.
He stroked my face. Kissed my cheek. His beard was scratchy—it hurt.
I tried to pull away.
He tightened his grip.
"New rule," he said. "Never pull away from me."
He rubbed my back. Asked if I was tired. I nodded. I was. So tired.
He laid me beside him on the couch. My legs rested across his lap. He
took off my sandals—white, beautiful sandals my mom had packed.
One landed upright. The other on its side.
Why do I remember that?

He rubbed my legs. My feet. His hands moved slowly. Then they moved in ways that felt wrong—ways I didn't understand, but that made me want to disappear. He told me to stay still. Told me not to pull away.

I hadn't even tried to.

I was silent. Completely silent.

He kept me there for what felt like hours. His hands moved over me like he owned me. At some point, my clothes were gone. I remember seeing them in a small pile on the floor. They looked like a tiny snowman. That's what I focused on—to keep from feeling anything else.

That was my first night.

He didn't hit me. But what he did? It didn't need a bruise to leave a mark. I didn't have words for it then. I barely have them now. But it echoed inside me for years.

When he was done, he told me to follow him. I remember hoping I was going to my own room. Somewhere to sleep. He led me to a small bedroom.

"This is where you'll sleep," he said.

The bed was small but big enough for a child. He opened one of the bags my mom had packed, pulled out a few of my nightgowns, and tossed them into the trash.

"You won't need those."

I stood there—confused. Naked. Unsure what I was supposed to do.

"It's time for bed," he said.

I climbed in.

This wasn't my bed. It was our bed.

He undressed. I closed my eyes. I felt the weight of him slide in beside me.

His skin against mine. He wrapped his arm around me, resting his hand where it didn't belong. Every so often, it moved slightly. Not enough to hurt. But enough to haunt me. I didn't fight. I just cried silently, facing the wall.

It became routine. If I heard him sit on the couch, I knew what was expected. Sometimes he didn't even touch me—I was just supposed to be there. Present. Available.

That's what I learned to be: available.

There's nothing I can say that makes this make sense.

There's no "lesson" I walked away with.

Or maybe... the lesson was this: Silence is safer than truth.

Chapter Seven: The Rules

Over the weeks, then months, of living in my "new home," I adjusted
to the routines.

Wake up. Brush my teeth. Sit on the sofa and wait.

Wait for what, you might ask?

I waited for him to tell me what to do next.

I'd hear him moving around in the kitchen. But I didn't dare move. I
made that mistake once—and I wasn't allowed to get up for the rest of
the day. And I mean all day. Just to make sure the lesson stuck, I even
had accidents right there on the sofa.

Sick, isn't it?

I learned quickly: do what you're told. Only what you're told.
Eventually, he would walk in and sit beside me, silent. Except for that
first day, when he laid out the rules, his voice calm, rehearsed, final:
"In the morning when you wake up, you'll have chores. First, brush
your teeth. Comb your hair. Be quiet. When you're done, sit on the
couch. DO NOT go anywhere else in the house. When I come in and
sit beside you, DO NOT look at me. DO NOT speak to me. When I
say okay, say, 'Good morning, Daddy.' Then you'll kneel in front of me,
between my legs. I'll kiss you good morning. Then you'll kiss him good
morning, until he wakes up. When I say okay, you'll stand up and say,
'Thank you, Daddy,' and go eat breakfast. Understood?"

"Yes, Daddy."

I didn't really understand who he was at the time. But I got to know
him well.

And in case you were wondering—yes, we were naked. Always naked.
Clothes, he said, were inconvenient in the house.

That was our morning routine. It never changed. If he was anything,
he was consistent.

After I told him good morning, I'd go to the table where breakfast
waited. Usually cereal or oatmeal. One time there were eggs and

sausage with toast, but the morning had gone long, and by the time I got to the plate, a few critters had found their way in. Cereal seemed safer after that.

After breakfast, I was allowed to color. Still naked, of course. And let me tell you, dining chairs on bare skin? Not comfortable. But I didn't care. I loved coloring. I would've sat on tacks if it meant being away from him.

If and when he called me, I dropped everything. I stood in front of him like a trained soldier.

"Yes, Daddy?"

Looking back now, I don't think he ever worked. He was always home. We were always alone.

Except when he threw parties.

Chapter Eight: Party Time

Content Warning: Child sexual abuse, coercion, grooming
There was a rhythm to my days back then. A strange, hollow rhythm.
Afternoons passed in silence, punctuated by the sound of his footsteps,
his voice, his needs. I had a few toys in a box, but I rarely used them.
When he wanted to play, I was the toy. That's just how it was.
It's hard to explain how quickly something unnatural can become
normal. I stopped questioning it. I stopped expecting anything else.
And then one day, he told me we were having a party.
I didn't know what that meant. But I smiled. I always smiled. He said
there would be people, rules, and that I was to look and act a certain
way. He gave me a dress—white, frilly, and much too formal for the
lonely life I had been living. My little white sandals didn't match, worn
and dirty, but I wore them proudly. They were all I had.
I remember feeling... excited. That's hard to admit now. But I hadn't
seen anyone else in months. I was just a child—lonely, hungry for any
version of attention, even if it came with rules.
There were so many rules.
Smile. Stay quiet. Obey without hesitation. Only leave with his
permission. Answer to no one. And never, ever forget who was in
charge.
The guests arrived slowly. Some faces I still see in dreams—smiling,
laughing, reaching. Most became a blur. But the house filled quickly
with noise, voices, footsteps, and eyes.
He tapped his glass and made a speech. Something about trust.
Something about celebration. I only remember one line:
"Tonight, we celebrate who we are, without judgment."
There was music. Loud and dizzying. He led me to the center of the
room and told me to dance. So I did. I spun and spun, my dress flaring
around me like a fragile halo. They clapped. They laughed.

Later, when I was tired, he placed me on the couch and told me to rest. But the night wasn't over.

That party became something else. Something far more sinister. Behind closed doors, the rules changed. Or maybe they didn't—and that was the point. I became a prize, passed around like a favor owed or a secret shared.

One by one, they came. Some smiled. Some didn't. A few tried to be gentle. Most didn't bother. The line between being used and being erased blurred quickly.

I don't remember all their names. Or maybe I never knew them. But I remember how each door closed behind them. I remember how he checked in, over and over, reminding me to be good. To smile.

And I did.

Because that's what I had learned to do. Smile, even when everything in me wanted to scream.

By morning, I was curled on a sofa, empty and aching. My body hurt. My mind floated somewhere else—above it all, disconnected. He stumbled in, drunk and angry, furious that I had given someone else what he believed belonged only to him. His cruelty that night was a punishment, a reminder. One I would never forget.

That was the first "party."

And somehow... it was one of the better nights.

Because things only got worse.

It's hard to believe there are people in this world capable of doing such things to children—but they exist. Some hide in plain sight.

And sometimes, even now, I find myself in disbelief... that I was that little girl.

Chapter Nine: The Holding Room

Content Warning: This chapter contains references to child sexual abuse, trafficking, and emotional dissociation. Details are conveyed in a non-graphic, trauma-informed way. Reader discretion is advised.

Over the next year, life didn't get better. It just got louder—darker—more consuming.

Everything that had become "normal" only escalated. The rules stayed the same, but the punishments, the expectations, the invasions of my body—they grew. Each day he tried something new, something worse, something he hadn't done the day before. Each time, I folded further inward—vanishing piece by piece. I learned how to escape in my mind. To float far away, even when my body stayed behind.

I rarely left the house—only for the parties.

There were five in total before it all stopped. I'm not going to talk about what happened at each one. Not yet. Not fully. I'll tell you about one. Because that one... was just like all the others.

Each party began the same way. I'd get a new dress. He'd do his best to brush my hair. I was supposed to look presentable—pretty, even. Like a doll. We would arrive, and I would be taken to a room right away. This room had toys. It always did.

Looking back, that was one of the most disturbing things—how carefully it was designed to look safe. Like a child's playroom. Bright colors, stuffed animals, blocks, dolls. But nothing about it was normal. It was a lie painted in pastels. I never touched the toys. I'd walk around the room quietly, just observing them—like they belonged to someone else. Someone who got to play and laugh and be a child. Not me.

After a while, the door opened. This time, there were other children. A boy, a little taller than me, walked in. Behind him, a girl. Younger. Smaller. I wanted to run to them—hug them, talk to them, anything. But I didn't. I knew the rules. I wasn't allowed to do anything unless I was told to.

The woman who brought them in didn't say a word. No names. No smiles. No introductions. She left as quickly as she came. The boy and girl didn't look surprised to see me. That shook me more than anything—how ordinary this seemed to them. I was shocked to see them. But they... weren't surprised at all. Like this had happened before.

We didn't speak. We just sat quietly on the floor, surrounded by toys that no one played with. We stayed there for what felt like hours. Then adults would come. Sometimes they'd take one of us. Sometimes two. And on a few occasions, all three. The memories blur from there. I won't go into what happened behind those closed doors—not now.

I'm not ready. But I will say this:

We were told what to do—to each other.

Sometimes they gave instructions.

Sometimes they simply watched.

And sometimes... they became part of it.

I remember hearing the little girl cry during one of those times. And my first thought wasn't, Is she okay? It was, She's going to get in trouble for that.

That's how deeply the rules had sunk into me.

At that same party, a woman came into the room and asked to see me. She took me aside, away from the others. But she didn't touch me. She just talked. She asked questions.

Where was I from?

How old was I?

Was the man I lived with my dad?

Where was my mommy?

Was I okay?

Did I need anything?

I answered everything. Calmly. Politely. Just like I'd been taught. Then she asked, "Do you want anything?"

And I said, "I want to go home."

She looked at me for a long time. Then she nodded and walked me back to the room.

I don't know why I told her the truth. Maybe part of me thought she could help. Maybe I just wanted someone to know.

But I remembered the rules.

And what came next would make sure I never forgot them again.

Chapter Ten: The Cost of Breaking Rules

Content Warning: This chapter contains references to child abuse, emotional manipulation, coercive control, and trauma. Written in a non-graphic, trauma-informed way. Reader discretion is advised.

That old saying, rules were meant to be broken, never applied to my life. In my world, rules were sacred. Breaking them meant consequences—always.

After we returned from that particular "party," things settled back into the usual routine. For a few days, everything was quiet. Familiar. Not safe—but familiar.

I never had a room of my own. Just a suitcase and a couple of duffle bags that held my things. I didn't even have a drawer. Some days, I didn't know if I was staying or leaving, and honestly, it didn't seem to matter.

Him was the only constant. The only person I had, even if the trust I had in him was warped by survival. I tried to follow every rule. I really did. But sometimes I forgot. Sometimes I made mistakes.

And for every mistake, there was a punishment.

He couldn't take away friends—I didn't have any.

He couldn't ground me from going outside—I never left.

He couldn't withhold treats—I wasn't given any.

He didn't even bother threatening to take away toys or clothes—I barely had either.

So instead, he gave me pain.

For small infractions, the punishments were "discipline drills":

I had to stand with both arms extended straight out to my sides.

I wasn't allowed to drop them, not even for a second.

If I did, he hit me, with his hand, or whatever he happened to be holding.

Another version was being made to squat against a wall, arms out in front. My legs and arms would burn, but I learned to prefer that one. At least I didn't have to look at him.
Once, for something more "serious," he made me stand in an ant bed. It wasn't long—but long enough. Long enough to hurt. Long enough to leave marks. That particular punishment only happened once, though. I had to stay "presentable" for his guests.
I rarely broke rules after that.
But a few days after the party, the one where I spoke to the woman, I was sitting naked at the dining table, coloring, when everything shifted again.
He yanked me from the chair by my hair. My body hit the ground hard, and I cried out.
He shouted about the rules.
How I had betrayed him.
How ungrateful I was.
How I had "failed the test."
He paced. Ranted. Laughed at times. I don't remember every word—but the rage in his voice stuck with me. I was just a child, but I was already very aware: this was not about rules. It was about control. Eventually, he dragged me to a room I'd never slept in before, the one with no windows.
There was no bed anymore. Just a cot and a sheet.
"This is where you'll stay until you learn your lesson," he said.
To him, this was punishment. But to me?
It was heaven.
I had a room to myself.
I didn't have to share a bed with him.
No touching. No pretending. Just silence.
It didn't even matter that there was no food. No water. No toilet. For the first few hours—maybe even the first day—I didn't care.
But then hunger set in. Thirst. Loneliness.

I remember waking up and realizing I hadn't seen him in over a day. I had to use the bathroom in the corner. I curled up in the sheet and tried to disappear.

Then the door opened.

But it wasn't him.

A man I had never seen before stepped in. I was nearly six and a half years old by then, and I knew something was different.

He held a glass of water in one hand and a muffin in the other.

He knelt down beside me, offered me the food and drink, and gently asked, "Are you okay?"

I didn't speak. I just nodded and devoured the muffin.

He asked questions—just like the woman had.

Where was I from?

Was I okay?

Was he my father?

This time, I didn't answer. I stayed quiet. But he didn't leave me there. He took me away. I never saw him again.

There are more memories. Some small. Some enormous. Scents that transport me. Details that stick for no reason. But that moment—that quiet rescue—was the turning point.

Years later, I would learn the truth behind everything. The reason I had ended up there.

There had been a deal. Money was tight.

I was traded. Loaned out. Like merchandise.

—

Chapter Eleven: Permission

I didn't know where I was going when the people came to pick me up. They packed what little I had left into a car, and we drove off. I must've been around six or maybe six and a half. Time felt like a blur.

I drifted in and out of sleep for most of the trip, the motion of the car rocking me like a cradle. But eventually, I started to recognize the roads. The shop. The trees. Home.

It felt like forever since I had seen this place, and for the first time in what felt like years, I felt something close to joy. I wondered briefly where he was, but the moment I saw the little store near the house, none of that mattered anymore.

When the car stopped, no one ran out to greet me.

The men who brought me just walked me up to the door, placed my bags down beside me, knocked, and left. I stood there, waiting.

Hopeful.

The door opened.

Cressida looked down at me, expressionless. "Well, grab your bags. Nothing has changed. You know where they go."

Just like that, my happiness was flattened. But I didn't let it sit long. I was too focused on one thing: finding my sister.

I searched the house, calling for her, but she was gone. So was my grandfather. My mother wasn't there either.

"Cressida, where is Noelle? Where's Mom?" I asked.

She placed her hands gently on my shoulders. "They live in Holland now."

There was something sad in her voice when she said it. It almost sounded like regret. I think, maybe, she missed them too.

Cressida never asked me where I had been. Never questioned who I had been with or what had happened. But she wasn't mean to me either. Not this time. She wasn't warm, but she wasn't cruel.

And that? That was enough for me.

After where I had just come from, the quiet indifference of my
grandmother felt like a blessing.

I went into the room my sister and I used to share. Her things were
gone. The space felt hollow without her, and somehow, I felt lonelier
than I ever had—even after years of isolation.

Cressida brought in my packed bags and set them in the room. "Get
what you need," she said. "Don't unpack. You won't be staying long."

I didn't understand what she meant. I didn't ask. I just nodded.

—-

One afternoon, I was sitting in the shop when a woman came by to sell
clothes. She had bags upon bags and chatted with my grandmother
outside before coming in.

"No, no—she's old enough to help," I heard Cressida say. "She just
came back from vacation not too long ago. She should be fully rested!"

She motioned for me. "Isla, come help with these bags, please."

I jumped up. Helping felt good. It made me feel useful.

The woman smiled kindly. "So, where did you go on vacation?"

I froze. My stomach flipped. I turned to look at Cressida.

"Well, answer," she said flatly. "She's talking to you."

I had no idea what to say. What could I say?

"Isla!" Cressida snapped.

I started crying—real, uncontrollable crying. The kind that comes
from somewhere deeper than words.

"Oh, don't cry," the woman said softly, her voice full of concern. It was
the kindest voice I'd heard in as long as I could remember.

Cressida waved it off. "She's just shy, that's all. She's fine. She was in
Europe."

Europe?

"She learned to ride horses and visited all sorts of neat places. Didn't
you, Isla?"

Through my tears, I answered, "Yes, Cressida."

I bent down, picked up the bags I could carry, and just stood there, waiting.

They kept talking.

Still, I stood.

"Well, take them inside," Cressida said. "What are you waiting for?"

"Permission," I replied.

There was silence—long enough to feel it settle in the air.

Finally, Cressida spoke, this time softer: "Take them inside."

As I walked past, I heard the woman ask, "Is she okay?"

"Yes," Cressida said. "She's just not used to doing anything for anyone else."

I turned back and looked at her.

And I smiled.

Chapter 12: The Good Doesn't Last

Content Warning: This chapter contains references to child sexual abuse, emotional neglect, and trauma-related memory loss. Reader discretion is advised.

I didn't stay long with Cressida. Maybe a few weeks. Just enough time to feel the ground under my feet again before it shifted.

My grandfather visited a few times a week, returning from trading trips. In the early mornings, he would make us coffee and we'd sit at the back of the house, watching the sunrise. Those were good memories—quiet ones I can still hold in my hands.

Then my mother came to take me to Holland.

Our reunion wasn't the kind that gets remembered for its warmth. It just happened. We went. No big emotions. No explanations. Just motion.

That's when I met Vernon—my new stepfather.

The house in Holland was unlike anything I'd ever known. A two-story home. My sister and I had our own rooms. Indoor plumbing. A television in the living room—and another one in my mom's room. It was the kind of place that made you think, maybe things will be different here. And in some ways, they were.

Vernon was friendly at first. Polite. Present. But I never felt like I belonged. He and my sister had a bond that had already been built while I was "away." I had been on the outside for so long that I didn't know how to step back in.

Our relationship was... functional. I wasn't treated badly, not at first. But it didn't feel like family. It felt more like I was a guest—or an assistant.

Still, I told myself: It's better than where I came from.

I had chores—lots of them. I used a step stool to reach the sink and wash dishes. My sister would come into the kitchen, drop her dirty

things in the sink, and walk away. She was never asked to help. My
mother never said anything about it.

She never really advocated for me.

I see that now—clearer through adult eyes.

Back then, I just tried to be helpful. To fit in. To stay quiet and
unnoticed.

But eventually, things shifted again.

I don't know exactly when it began. I've blocked out the specifics, and
maybe that was my mind protecting me. But I remember that, little by
little, Vernon began to break boundaries.

He would come into my room when no one was watching.
Sometimes, when I was trying to sleep. Other times, he found ways to
isolate me—under the pretense of chores or supervision.

There was one night that stands out.

I had been told to wait to clean the kitchen until after my mother and
sister went to bed. So I sat quietly, watching him watch TV. Hours
passed before he gave me permission to begin. When I finished, he
checked my work, praised it, then directed me to the living room.
What followed wasn't new to me. I had been trained in silence and
expectation long ago. But this time, it came with something new:
intimidation. A symbol of power and control placed nearby. A threat
that didn't have to be spoken aloud.

And in that moment, I thought I saw something—or someone.

A flash of my mother in the hallway.

Watching.

Then walking away.

After that night, something changed in me. I was no longer just
obedient, I was scared.

At dinner one evening, I spilled my drink because I was trembling.
When I saw him walk into the room, I panicked and ran to hide under
the table.

He pulled me out without a word, threw me over his shoulder, and carried me upstairs. My mother was shouting, telling him to stop. He didn't even look at her.

As we climbed the stairs, everything in my memory goes dark.

I don't remember what happened. Or maybe I can't. Or won't.

Days later, we packed up our things and went back to Maranza.

No one talked about it.

No one asked me how I felt.

Another ending I was told was my fault.

Another place I didn't belong.

I've tried to understand why I can't remember. Maybe it's because part of me doesn't want to. Maybe that memory would break something I've only just started to mend. Or maybe it's because I already knew what happened. And naming it would make it too real.

I don't know what I don't know.

But I do know this: good things never seemed to last.

And somewhere along the way, I began to believe that was my fault.

I had been told enough times that if I hadn't been born, life would've been better for everyone else.

And it's hard not to carry that belief when it's sewn into the fabric of your childhood.

Chapter 13: Almost Safe

We didn't stay in Maranza long. Before I knew it, we were on our way to Southport.

I don't remember much about our time there—at least not anything troubling. We lived in an apartment with my Uncles, and my grandparents. My mom worked two jobs. My sister and I were enrolled in a Catholic school.

Eventually, my mom, sister, and I moved into our own place. My mom was gone most of the time, working. Noelle and I were usually left alone. And still, even in that quiet... nothing bad happened.

No one hurt me.

No one mistreated me.

No one made me feel unsafe.

It was the calmest stretch I'd had in years.

After a few months, the entire family relocated again—this time to Greyford, Caldera. My mom had gone ahead of us, and by the time we arrived, she had already married my new stepfather: Micah.

I loved Micah immediately.

He told us we could call him Dad, and I didn't hesitate. I wanted to. I wanted that word to mean something good.

He showed me affection in the way I had longed for—not just attention, but warmth. We'd watch TV together. On cold nights, we'd share a blanket. It wasn't complicated. It wasn't confusing.

It was love—and I felt safe.

When my mom introduced us to Micah, I was ecstatic. You'd think I'd be hesitant or shy—but I wasn't. Not at all. I was all in from the very beginning. I wanted his love and approval so badly. I called him Daddy right away, even though my sister refused. She often told me not to call him that, reminding me that our real dad was in Maranza. But in my heart, I had room for both. Truthfully, I had room for anyone who could and would love me. My sister didn't call him Dad at first. But over time, she did. I think she loved him too.

Before I go further into our life in the Greyford, I need to take you back to a time in Maranza. This is a story my sister often shared as a hurt in her life. Looking back, I don't know if it's truly her memory or one she absorbed through years of our mother telling it. Either way, it became part of our story.

Before I was born, my mom married my dad, and they had my sister. By all accounts, it could've been a fairytale. My father's family was one of the wealthiest in Maranza. My sister was adored and always beautifully dressed. My mom, young and striking, had seemingly gone from modest roots to a life of comfort and prestige. Against his family's wishes, my father married her—but according to my mother, they never accepted her. She said she was treated like an outsider, never truly welcomed into their circle. Whether that's entirely true, I don't know. Over the years, I've come to doubt many of the stories I was told.

Whatever the truth may be, their marriage didn't last. My mother said she was already pregnant with me when they separated. Maybe that was part of the reason they ended. I never got the full story growing up—just fragments. Some truths came much later, closer to my father's death—but that story belongs in another chapter.

By the time I was born, my mother and sister had returned to my grandparents' home. My father never came around. We didn't live like the daughters of a prince, but like the daughters of a pauper. The story goes that he'd pass us playing outside and never even slow down. My sister says she'd wave, but he never acknowledged us. I learned more about that much later.

I share this now to help explain something I struggled to understand as a child. Around the age of seven, I was confused by my sister's refusal to call Micah "Dad." Our real dad wasn't in our lives—so why couldn't we love the man who was? Maybe she didn't need the kind of love I was desperate for. But I did. And Micah became my dad. He gave me the love I craved, and I loved him in return—fiercely, completely.

Micah was, and still is, a quiet man. He didn't need much to be happy. He would take us on walks and talk about animals, trees, the stars. He always seemed to know a little bit about everything. He built a mud fort in the backyard with me, and I'd line up my little green army men while he launched mud bombs at them. We made beautiful memories. I'm so grateful for that time.

By the time my brother was born, I was eleven. Like I've said before—it was a glorious time. Not long after, my baby sister followed. Having them in my life brought me a kind of peace I hadn't known. They were innocent. Pure. Having children of his own now, I faded into the background. The outsider.

But I didn't mind—not really. Because I adored them, especially my brother.

He became the center of my world. His smile, his laugh, his tiny hands reaching for mine—it was enough.

He made me feel like maybe I could be the protector.

Like maybe love didn't have to disappear.

My mom had never been a nurturing mother. So I poured all my love—the love I had bottled up for years—into my baby brother and little sister. Sometimes life takes so much from us... and then, just when we're gasping for breath, it places a gift at our feet. Something we needed, exactly when we needed it.

But peace has never lasted long for me.

Chapter 14: The Weight Of Worth

Before we continue on with where life took us, I wanted to take a moment to share this with you: After everything I'd already been through, life finally seemed to be getting better, at least on the surface. The biggest pain I felt during this time didn't come from strangers. It came from my grandmother's constant, cutting comments, and later, from my own mother. She joined in. That pain still lives in me.

It always felt like my mother only loved me in private. She would hug me behind closed doors and tell me how others in the family said horrible things about me. But always, always, she would reassure me, "I stand up for you." And I believed her, I was a child.

But over time, the mistrust I already carried from years of abandonment and betrayal only deepened. It never healed.

My mother would tell me who disliked me, and then take me around those same people, smiling and laughing like nothing was wrong. I was instructed not to treat them differently. Not to say anything. To keep her secrets and pretend I was fine.

I was constantly confused. Constantly conflicted. And I never, ever trusted anyone fully, not even her. I share this with you now, because this is where most of us get the idea of our worth. And when you are shown repeatedly and told repeatedly that you are worthless, it becomes your truth.

Chapter 15: What Was Taken, What Was Given

One evening, as my brother played on the shaggy carpet, Micah and I sat under our blanket watching television. My mother passed through the room more than once. She didn't say anything, but we felt it—her discontent thick in the air. I waited. I was always waiting. Life had made me hypervigilant.

Then she stepped in front of us, her finger pointing, her voice rising. "You're a no-good son of a bitch! You think I don't know what you're doing under that blanket? You have her touching you, don't you!?"

Everything slowed.

Micah's face was a storm of horror, hurt, and disbelief. He looked at me—his eyes searching—and I was crying. Without a word, he threw the blanket off and walked out of the room. I can't remember if he said anything. I just remember the silence. And my mother's eyes on me.

"And you!" she hissed. "You like it, don't you!?"

I was eleven.

And if I could go back—if I could crash through time like a storm—I would run into that room and stand in front of her. I would scream, "STOP! ENOUGH! You don't get to twist love into something shameful. You don't get to break the only safe thing I had!"

I would gather that little girl into my arms, hold her so tightly, and whisper what no one else ever did: "You did nothing wrong. You were just trying to feel safe. To feel loved. None of this was your fault."

I couldn't protect her then. But I can now. And I will—word by word, page by page.

That was the last time Micah and I ever watched TV together under a blanket. The last time we sat on the same sofa.

A year later, my baby sister was born. Up until then, I had been the baby girl, at least in my own mind. I was twelve now, and jealousy did creep in. I'm not proud of it. I should've been out with friends, being a kid. But instead, I was trying every day to be a better daughter, to feel like I belonged. I just wanted something—anything—that felt real. And this? This didn't feel real anymore.

Somehow, I convinced myself it was my fault.

Chapter 16: Consistently Inconsistent

After my little sister was born, life was relatively peaceful for a while. I was twelve. My oldest sister, Elara, was completely immersed in caring for the new baby, and before long, my mother, Corva, became just as captivated.

Up until then, I had been the baby girl, at least in my own mind. I was twelve now, and jealousy did creep in. I'm not proud of it. I should've been out with friends, being a kid. But instead, I was trying every day to be a better daughter, to feel like I belonged. I just wanted something—anything—that felt real.

I found myself mostly on the outside, observing. I couldn't always process what I was feeling—it wasn't confusion exactly, but a constant effort to understand people and their behavior. I watched the way my mother protected my youngest sister. Sometimes she stepped in before there was even a need, especially when it came to discipline. If my dad so much as raised his voice, Corva was already there, claiming he was too harsh or unfair.

Later, when my sister wasn't around, Corva would say things that left me with questions I didn't know how to answer. She suggested my father resented the baby because she was too strong-willed to be manipulated or harmed. I remember those moments vividly—not just the words, but the way they lingered, unsettling and hard to grasp. It made me wonder: did she believe the opposite about me? That I was easier to manipulate? That I invited mistreatment simply by being too agreeable? I didn't think I had done anything wrong. I was a quiet, well-behaved kid. I never caused trouble. I couldn't bear the thought of disappointing anyone, especially my parents. I didn't just avoid consequences—I avoided conflict altogether. I lived for approval.

I noticed how my dad lit up around my little brother. He was warm and playful with him, the way he used to be with me—before everything changed. At some point, a kind of fear crept into the way he interacted with us. Like he didn't know what was safe anymore. But with my brother, that tension seemed to ease.

At the time, we were living in Caldera. My dad's family was in Riverhall, and when he got a job offer there that paid three times more than what he was making, he took it. Surprisingly, Corva agreed to the move, even though her family was all still in Caldera.

It was another big shift. While I didn't have many friends in Caldera, I had grown comfortable there. Cressida and my grandfather were nearby too. But in truth, putting distance between me and Cressida felt like a relief. When she and Corva were together, it created a heaviness I couldn't describe—like I needed to disappear just to breathe.

My dad went ahead to Riverhall and found us a beautiful townhouse in a quiet neighborhood. When we arrived, it felt like stepping into a dream. Everything was new—fresh carpet, clean blinds, and we even had a dishwasher. From our balcony, you could see trees stretching toward the sky and a little glimmer of a pond in the distance.

Each of us had our own bedroom—except for the youngest two, who still shared. My mom's room was the most elegant in the house. My dad had picked out a floral comforter and arranged everything with care. It looked like something out of a magazine. Even though the living and dining areas were still bare, he made sure Corva's room was warm and inviting—a sanctuary.

Despite all the changes, the beauty of that place stirred something in me. Maybe hope. Maybe just the wonder of having something new. But underneath it all, I still held my breath. Always watching. Always waiting.

With my dad's new job came long hours, and he was gone most of the day until late in the evening. My mother grew convinced he was having an affair. She didn't keep it to herself—she made sure we all knew what she suspected. She reminded us often that people couldn't be trusted. What she didn't realize was that I already carried that belief deep inside me.

Elara and I started school in Riverhall with no new clothes. Our cousins brought bags of hand-me-downs, which became our wardrobe. There's nothing wrong with hand-me-downs, but for girls starting over in a new school, wearing mismatched outfits was a bit humiliating. Still, we never complained. We were taught to be grateful, so we were.

We had arrived in the coldest part of the year. Coming from Caldera, snow was still a novelty—and not a pleasant one. We didn't have snow boots or proper winter coats. To keep our feet dry, we tied Walmart bags around our shoes, but by the time we got to school, our socks were soaked and freezing.

Elara never said much about how she felt at her new high school, and neither did I. But if I endured daily bullying, I'm sure she did too. She fit in more than I did—tall, with beautiful green eyes, porcelain skin, and perfectly styled hair. I, on the other hand, was short with wild hair and a darker complexion than most of the kids at school. People told me to "go back where I came from" and knocked books from my hands. Once, I wore a skirt to school, and a group of boys surrounded me, taunting me in a way that still makes my stomach twist. I felt hated. I felt alone.

Neither of us wanted to go anywhere after school. Home—uncertain as it was—felt safer than the world outside.

Eventually, my mom grew tired of the isolation. Thankfully, my dad's brother, Silas, was outgoing and often took her out during the day to run errands. Simple outings, like grocery shopping, seemed to lift her spirits. So much so, in fact, that my dad noticed. Not long after, Silas moved into our basement.

That was the beginning of the end.

While we lived in Riverhall, we never did anything as a family. My mother told us our dad was ashamed to be seen with us. Whether or not it was true, it was easy to believe. It made it easier to hate everything about that place. Eventually, Elara and I started begging to move back to Caldera. To our surprise, Corva agreed—but only on one condition.

Silas would come with us.

And our dad could never find out we were leaving.

I had assumed we'd all be going together. When I realized that wasn't the plan, I was torn. My mother wanted me to keep secrets from my father—life-altering secrets. I never wanted to be the kind of person who could be manipulated, who betrayed people. I wanted to be different from the dysfunction I came from. But there I was, helping to carry it out.

Corva told us she was in love with Silas and that he would be leaving with us. The plan was to wait until my dad left for work, pack our things into a U-Haul, and disappear before he came home. My heart broke. I asked if we could at least call him at work to say goodbye.

"Absolutely not," she said.

"Can I leave him a letter?"

"No. Nothing. We are not leaving anything behind."

I was stunned. Then she softened her voice, placing a hand on my shoulder.

"Don't you want me to be happy?" she asked.

And in that moment, I realized—I did. Her happiness had always meant more to me than my own. More than my pain, more than my loyalty, more than my father's heartbreak. What she needed from me had always outweighed what I needed from her.

As the day approached, I hugged my dad more than I ever had. Knowing what I knew, it felt like I was betraying him with every embrace. I felt like a traitor. Just like the people I'd vowed never to become.

The morning of our departure, my dad left for work around 5:30 a.m. He kissed my mother and said he'd see us later. If only he knew, I thought. As he headed down the stairs, I ran outside after him. My mom yelled at me to come back. Maybe she thought I was going to confess everything. But I knew better. My dad might have left us, but my mother would never let me go. I couldn't trust he'd stay in my life if she wasn't in it. But she would always be there.

She was consistently inconsistent. It was the only consistency I knew.

Chaos.

By 6:30, the U-Haul was in the front yard. We scrambled to load the few things we could take. My little brother and sister thought it was a grand adventure. The phone rang a couple of times while we were packing. We couldn't answer it. I wanted to. Desperately.

We left before 2:00 that afternoon. I kept watching the time, knowing exactly when my dad would be home. I wondered how he would feel. My heart ached for him. I promised myself I'd never do this to anyone else.

It was a promise I didn't keep.

So many thoughts ran through my mind as we drove away.

Does he hate me now?

Will he think this was my fault?

Will he come find us?

What happens now?

My mother often said that history repeats itself. I've carried that warning like a weight. I still have nightmares—not just about what happened, but about becoming the people I tried so hard not to be. I put up a good fight. But some days, I look in the mirror and catch glimpses of them staring back.

It's a struggle every day—to feel like I belong, to grow where I'm planted.

But it can be done.

—

Chapter 17: The Weight of Silence

The drive back to Caldera felt longer than I remembered—maybe because of all the thoughts racing through my mind. I watched the way my mom interacted with Silas. It was different from how she had been with my dad. She seemed happier, lighter. But Silas was someone new. The new will wear off, I thought to myself.

It was almost as if she wanted to reinvent herself—shed the past and become someone different. Maybe she believed she could.

I stared out the window, watching the scenery blur by. My little brother and sister were well-behaved on the trip, playing quietly with the few toys we'd set aside for the long road home. My oldest sister had a Walkman and spent most of the drive listening to music. From time to time, she'd glance over and smile at me. She didn't have to say anything. That smile said everything: We're going to be okay.

But I wasn't sure we would be. I couldn't stop thinking about my dad and the pain he must have felt—walking into his home and finding everyone he loved gone. And his own brother gone too. The betrayal must have been devastating.

I wish I had been stronger.

We stayed in a hotel for a few days before finding a place to rent. It was a nice house, and once again, a new beginning. Eventually, we got a phone, and after months of silence, my dad was finally able to talk to us. Hearing his voice after all that time—it was heart-wrenching. You could hear the pain in every word.

When the conversations between my parents grew intense, we kids were sent out of the room. But the walls weren't thick. I heard things I didn't understand yet, things that made my chest tighten.

Eventually, the tension seemed to fade. My dad began calling more often to talk to us. Silas was kind, present, and careful. He wasn't our dad, and he never tried to be. He didn't discipline us or force closeness.

He was just a man who loved our mom—He grew to love us, and we grew to love him too.

That doesn't mean I let my guard down. I never could. Because one thing was always certain in my life: Uncertainty

Now, let me be clear—how this all happened was never good. But somehow, within our home, there was a fragile peace. A quiet we clung to in a world full of chaos we couldn't change.

Almost a year went by before our dad was able to visit. The plan was to meet him at a park. He'd spend the day with us, then drop us off afterward. He said he'd be in town for a couple of days. I was so excited. I was older now—maybe he wasn't expecting how happy I'd be to see him. The moment I felt his arms around me, it was like breathing again. He kissed me on the head and hugged my little brother and sister. I turned to wave to my mom by the car, ready to run back to my dad.

She motioned me over.

I ran to her, still smiling, eager to go back.

"Tell him goodbye. You're not staying."

The look on my face must have said it all.

"What? Why?"

She raised an eyebrow and smirked. "Isla, you're too big to play in the park."

"I just want to spend time with Dad," I said.

"He's not your dad," she replied flatly, and got into the car.

I ran back to my father, desperate, hoping he would change her mind.

"Dad, Mom said I can't stay!"

He pulled me into a hug and whispered, "I'm sorry. I hoped we could spend time together soon."

And that was it.

It felt like the air had been knocked out of me. I kissed my little brother and sister goodbye and watched as they walked away with him. Micah never returned my little brother and sister to us after the play date. If I had known that would be the last time I'd see them for at least two years, I would have never left.

I've often replayed that moment in my mind—the look in his eyes, the weight of goodbye. At the time, I thought heartbreak was something you got over. But I've learned that some goodbyes echo for years, growing heavier the longer they go unanswered. When my dad said he was sorry, I heard the words—but I didn't feel seen. I felt dismissed, discarded. At that moment, love seemed to flow only one way—from me to him. And even the most innocent gesture, like not fighting harder to keep me, felt like betrayal. I think people assume children are shaped in their earliest years, but I believe we're shaped again and again, especially those of us raised in the shadows of trauma. Something shifted in me that day. I began to understand that I could be wanted by no one, owned by everyone, and powerless to change either. He couldn't make me stay, even if he wanted to. My mother had likely made that very clear. And so, once again, I became someone different—someone who learned that even love has limits.

—

Chapter 18: Becoming Who They Needed

There wasn't a specific day I noticed myself disappearing. It happened quietly—like a soft erosion you don't feel until you try to stand, and your legs won't hold you.

By then, Silas had settled in fully. The peace in our home was fragile but consistent, and that alone felt like a gift. Corva seemed more relaxed. The chaos from before had been replaced with new routines. I wasn't afraid—but I wasn't exactly safe either. There was always an invisible thread of expectation, and I never wanted to be the one to snap it.

I started to measure my worth by how helpful I could be—how much space I didn't take up. I anticipated everyone's needs before they were spoken. If something needed doing, I was already halfway through it.

It wasn't that anyone told me I had to. It just became who I was.

The truth is, I wasn't taught how to be a person—I was taught how to be useful.

Even my quietness was a kind of currency. The less I needed, the more peace there was. The more I gave, the more likely I'd be noticed—not celebrated, but tolerated. A smile, a nod, a small thank-you could carry me through the day like a prize I'd won for being invisible.

My older sister had her own life by then. And it felt like she was allowed to have it. No one said it outright, but the permission was there, unspoken. She could exist for herself. I wasn't given that same space. I was still expected to serve, to listen, to carry what others dropped. Especially my mother.

She filled my ears with stories of what others thought of me—how our family didn't trust me, how they didn't want me around their children, how I was seen as promiscuous. I hadn't done anything to deserve those labels, but I believed them. When you're told you're unwanted by the people who should love you, and the only person who "cares" about you is the one feeding you the lie—you cling to them for survival.

And then she'd take me around those same family members and tell me, "Be nice. Don't say anything. They wouldn't believe you anyway."

That was the worst part. The pretending. The knowing. The silence.

So I said nothing. And it broke something in me.

Then, one day, everything shifted.

We were going to meet my dad, brother, and sister at a diner about thirty miles away. I remember how excited we were—how good it felt to be reunited. My mom had this beautiful classic car, and I always loved riding in it. As we pulled into the lot, I could already see them through the big glass window.

I didn't wait for the car to stop. I jumped out and ran straight into the diner.

It was pure joy. I threw my arms around them—touching their faces, kissing them, soaking in the sound of their laughter. Even now, sometimes a smell takes me back to that diner. The scent of syrup, leather seats, warmth, and comfort.

We ate, we laughed. We were a family again, if only for a little while.

As we were getting ready to leave, I asked if I could start the car. My mom handed me the key, and I ran out the door, still buzzing with happiness. I slid into the driver's seat, turned the ignition—and the key snapped off in my hand.

Just like that, everything changed.

We couldn't get home. We couldn't call Silas. We didn't even call her family—who lived just five or ten minutes away. Instead, we got a motel room.

My mom and dad shared the bed. The rest of us made a pallet on the floor.

We didn't call Silas that night. Or the next morning. When we finally returned home, he was furious. They argued all night. The yelling got

louder and louder until it turned physical. He slapped my mother.
And just like that, the relationship was over.
My dad took my little brother and sister back with him. Thank God
they weren't there to witness it.
My mom cried in the aftermath, and my sister and I went to comfort
her. I remember kneeling beside her, wrapping my arms around her
shoulders, trying to be enough. Trying to soothe her.
And then she turned to me and said,
"This is all your fault. You did this. You just don't want me to be
happy."
Then she turned away and hugged my sister.
My sister gave me the same tired look as always—part empathy, part
resignation. A silent message: Just ignore her. It's what she does.
But I didn't ignore it. I never could.
Those words opened a door in my mind, and all the old poison rushed
in. The day Cressida said "she was born," the whispers of shame, the
accusations of being unwanted, unworthy. Every seed she had ever
planted bloomed all at once.
And yet—I didn't get angry.
I got determined.
I told myself that from that day forward, I would prove her wrong.
That I could make her happy.
That she would see, eventually, all I ever cared about was her.

—-

I've carried that vow for years.
To prove her wrong. To make her proud. To make her happy—no
matter what it took. And I've bent myself in ways I didn't even know
were possible. I've stayed silent when I should've screamed. I've taken
blame that never belonged to me. I've given parts of myself I didn't
know I was allowed to keep.

And somewhere along the way, I forgot how to want things. I forgot how to exist outside of service, outside of guilt, outside of her shadow.

Even now, I sometimes feel that familiar grip tightening around my choices, around my joy. The voice in my head that whispers, "This is all your fault." I know better now. But the echoes don't always care what I know.

Still... I'm learning.

That love shouldn't require my silence.

That happiness doesn't have to be earned through pain.

That I was never broken—just bent into someone else's idea of who I should be.

And I am slowly, quietly, becoming someone else.

Someone I can recognize.

Chapter 19: The Doors Were Always Open

The doors were always open for me to come and go as I pleased. But unspoken words kept me where I was. I was a prisoner—not by locks or bars, but by something more invisible. A kind of jail I may have created myself. Hidden boundaries I just couldn't cross. Wouldn't cross.

I say my sister had a choice to build a life of her own—and she did. But I also had a choice. Still, something kept me there. A pull I couldn't explain. I felt like if I left, I would be failing my mother somehow. And failure, in my mind, meant losing love.

If I did make friends, I couldn't go to their houses. Occasionally, I'd invite them to mine. My mom was a gracious host—funny, radiant, charming. My friends loved her. She made people laugh, made them feel welcome. But the moment they left, everything changed.

"She's not welcome here again," my mother would say.

"She's trash. I can't believe you're friends with someone like that."

Over time, I stopped inviting anyone over at all.

Looking back now, I see the grooming. The psychological isolation. I was alienated from everyone—while still standing in the same room. My mom wanted me all to herself, and she used every tactic she could to prove that she was all I'd ever have.

And her plan worked.

Because I believed her.

I believed that people hated me. That others thought the absolute worst of me. That I was only tolerated, never truly liked. She told me these things out of concern. That she was just protecting me.

She said she was the only one who really loved me.

And I believed her—because I was starving to believe someone could.

I was starving for affection. And when you're starving, you'll eat anything. Even lies.

Sometimes, I thought about him. Not often. But when the memories came, they filled me with a hollow ache. Sadness. Confusion.

Questions I never felt allowed to ask.

Why did she leave me?

There was one afternoon I remember vividly. My mom was resting on the sofa, her eyes closed as I massaged her feet. The house was quiet.

The timing felt right. I had rehearsed my words silently, over and over, unsure how to ask without causing a storm.

"Mom... do you remember our trip on the bus?"

Her eyes flew open. She yanked her foot from my hands, sat upright, and glared.

"You always ruin everything, don't you?" she snapped.

"You just can't let me enjoy one moment without starting your bullshit."

She stood up and walked to her room, slamming the door behind her.

The next morning, I made her breakfast and had it waiting at the table. She came in, sat down, and still looked angry.

"I'm sorry, Mom," I said quietly.

She didn't respond.

But she ate.

So I counted it as a victory.

—-

The voice in my head wouldn't let up:

You're selfish. You hurt her feelings.

Why can't you just let things go?

That moment marked another shift in me. I started questioning everything.

Maybe what I had been through wasn't that bad.

Maybe I was overreacting.

Maybe I was the problem.
Maybe I was to sensitive.
Too soft.
Too weak.
And eventually, I believed all these things.

—-

My days were simple: school, then home. Sometimes, my mom and I would walk to my grandmother's house. I didn't like going—but I did look forward to seeing my grandfather.

He had emphysema by then, and he was mostly bedridden. Too weak to do much more than lie back and watch old Westerns on the TV. I would sit beside him, quietly watching whatever was on, grateful just to be near him. Those visits were the only thing that made the trip bearable.

On one particular visit, he had fallen asleep. So I stepped outside and sat on the porch to pass the time. When I came back up the stairs, I heard my mom's voice drifting from the living room.

I paused.

I knew what would happen if I got caught listening. But I stayed anyway.

Maybe I just wanted to hear someone say something kind about me. Maybe I hoped to learn what made people happy. Or maybe I was just tired of being in the dark. Either way, I listened.

At first, the conversation was about my uncles and their wives. Then I heard my grandmother ask, "Have you heard from your other two?"

She meant my brother and sister.

Then came the question that made my breath catch.

"Has Isla gotten any better?"

Better at what?

My mother answered without hesitation. "She stays out late all the time. I wouldn't be surprised if she ended up pregnant before she graduates. She's lazy—I have to do everything myself."

Cressida's voice followed. "I told you this would happen."

"She's ungrateful."

That word echoed in my chest like a drum.

Then I heard that my uncle didn't want me around his wife—said I might introduce her to bad things.

What bad things? I thought.

What have I done?

I crept quietly back down the stairs and sat on the porch again. My heart was too full to beat. My thoughts were too loud to hear.

When my mom finally came down, we walked home in silence—at least for a while.

Then she spoke.

"Your cousins have been saying awful things about you," she said. "But don't worry—I stood up for you. I made sure to tell your grandmother you're a good girl."

I smiled and said, "I know."

But something inside me turned off that day. I stopped feeling the way I used to.

Why? Why? Why?

What did I do that made my own mother incapable of loving me?

There must've been something deeply wrong with me.

And then I remembered.

I was born.

—-

Looking back now, it all feels almost surreal. As I write these words—as I read them back—it's like watching someone else's life unfold. And yet, it was mine. Every moment. Every sting. Every silence.

I didn't realize just how deep the wounds ran until I began to tell the truth out loud. The manipulation, the alienation, the sheer weight of trying to earn love—it's overwhelming to see it in black and white. And what shakes me most is how much I normalized it at the time. There's a kind of heartbreak in remembering. But there's also a strange, quiet strength in finally seeing it clearly. I survived this. That little girl—starving for affection, clinging to whatever scraps of love she could find—she's still here. And now, she's being heard.

Chapter 20: What I See Now

Writing this memoir—then reading it back—has been more than a process. It's been a reckoning.

It's one thing to live through something. It's another thing entirely to revisit it, to immerse yourself in those moments as you try to tell the story. And in doing so, I've come face-to-face with truths I had tucked away to survive.

There were times while writing that I found myself softening the edges. Trying to make the situations not look so bad. I would think, "Was that really so terrible?" or "Don't say that. They'll never forgive you." Even now, I repeat a quiet mantra in my head—"Your mom loves you. She loves you. She loves you."—as if the repetition could make it all easier to swallow.

She's older now. More fragile. And I feel guilty for writing this truth—as if I'm the reason she's not at peace in her old age.

But I didn't take her peace.

And I didn't take her love.

I just never had either one to begin with.

The psychological hold she has on me still lives in the corners of my mind. And I'm just now starting to turn the lights on.

While some people might have grown angry or bitter after what I endured, I became the opposite—soft, forgiving, patient.

But at what cost?

What the emotional abuse did to me has left a longer, deeper scar than any physical blow ever could. The manipulation—the constant erosion of truth and worth—was impossible to see for what it was, because it was normal. That was my everyday life.

The kinds of comments that would make another child cry or shrink in fear were background noise to me. If someone had told me back then, "This isn't how it's supposed to be," I would've thought they were the crazy one.

I believed everything I was told—about myself, about others, about what love looked like. I didn't even know I could question it.
It wasn't until much later that I started asking the hard questions:
Why can't I sustain a good relationship?
Why do I feel anxious around people?
Why didn't I keep childhood friends?
Why do I close myself off from the world—yet feel emotionally starved?
Why don't I feel safe... even in my own home?
Even now, I run when things feel too comfortable. Peace feels unfamiliar—chaotic moments make more sense to my nervous system.
When I fail, I want to give up.
When I let someone down, I feel like I could just disappear.
I don't know how to do things just for me.
That's selfish, right? At least, that's what I was taught.
But I'm starting to see it all clearly now.
And maybe, for the first time, I understand why I am the way I am.
This memoir is not just a telling of what happened.
It's a reclaiming. A remembering. A refusal to let the past steal the present.
These things happened to me—but they are not me.
I became a mother determined to give my children a different life. I supported them, celebrated them, stood beside them in all things. I cheered for their smallest accomplishments like they were gold medals.
I gave them what I never had.
But I still question myself.
Did I go too far in the other direction?
Did I overcompensate?
Did I hinder them with my overprotection?
I don't know. Maybe I'll always wonder.
But I do know this:

Every day, I try.
Every day, I show up.
And every day, I carry the hope that healing is still possible.
Even if the little girl inside me never got to feel safe—
the woman I am now is learning how to hold her close
and remind her:
You survived. You are worthy. And you were never the problem.

Chapter 21: Something Like Belonging

Life carried on as usual in the months leading up to my sister's graduation. I stayed close to my mom, doing what I could to ease her burdens. On occasion, we'd attend family gatherings—though gatherings always stirred something uneasy in me. I didn't have a word for it then, but looking back, I know it was anxiety. I would stay quiet, hover at the edges, and most often be put in charge of the little cousins. That suited me just fine. Children were predictable. Safe.

Then came the invitation from my dad in Maranza.

He wanted us to visit—just me and my sister. He sent money for clothes and tickets. I was elated.

Even though my sister and I weren't particularly close, we had an unspoken bond. I always felt I could count on her, and that comforted me. She was reserved, cautious. I was open, eager, emotional. She'd roll her eyes at my clinginess, telling me to calm down. But still—there was love between us.

When we arrived in Maranza, a man holding a sign with our name greeted us. My dad's driver. I was stunned. A driver? My sister explained that's just what people with money did.

As we pulled up to my dad's home—gated, with a circular driveway—I felt like I had stepped into a movie. My dad emerged from the upper balcony with open arms.

"My girls are finally here!" he called.

I dropped everything and ran.

My sister, as always, stayed composed, walking slowly behind me. We were just different that way.

The week that followed was like a dream. Boat rides, dinners out, shopping trips where things were simply put "on a tab." For once, we felt special. Seen. Taken care of.

It was one of the best weeks of my life.

And then, the night before we left, something happened I've never forgotten.

As I lay in bed, the door opened quietly. I saw my dad's figure enter the room. My heart raced. A flash of fear passed through me—please not you too.

But he simply lay beside me, wrapped his arms around me, and cried. "I'm so sorry, Isla," he whispered, over and over. "I love you so much. I'm so sorry."

He held me as he wept. Not for minutes—for a long time. He kissed my forehead and left.

We never spoke of it again.

But that moment—that night—became a touchstone. Proof that, somewhere in the mess of everything, love had existed. That maybe I had been loved, even if imperfectly. That memory has pulled me back from the edge more times than I can count.

My dad loved me. And for that one night, I felt it.

But nothing good ever seemed to last. Years later, someone would tell me that I had ruined his life too.

And just like that, another place I thought was mine... would slip away.

Chapter 22: After the Magic

Once my sister left, I didn't realize what her presence alone had been saving me from.

Day-to-day life didn't change all that much—at least not on the surface. But something had shifted in the air. The restraint that once existed was gone. Now, there was no holding back the verbal jabs, the opinions, the constant echoes of how others supposedly saw me. Even in the silence, I couldn't escape it. A tape played over and over in my head: You're worthless. You'll never be enough.

But it was never her voice directly. It was always "what other people said." She made sure to remind me how she was only trying to protect me, how I should be grateful for her honesty. As if love was wrapped in shame and warnings. I wasn't physically abused, and at the time, I didn't understand that what I was enduring was abuse. I was being groomed—to know my place, to shrink, to stay.

Did she know what she was doing?

Surely not. Right?

She loved me. She was all I had.

A year passed. My sister and I wrote letters, talked on the phone. She sounded lighter, more vibrant—her voice no longer weighed down.

There was a world out there that she had entered, and she was beginning to bloom. Every letter she sent became a treasure. Until one didn't.

One afternoon, I rushed to my room with a new envelope, heart pounding, eager to hear what she'd share next. But this letter was different. Her handwriting was the same, but the tone wasn't.

"Isla, you can't treat Mom the way you've been. Stop being rude to her. She doesn't deserve it. Now that I'm not there, you have to step up and help, not make things worse. Mom has gone through so much for us. You owe it to her to treat her with respect. Please calm down."

I froze. My eyes read it again. And again.

What was she talking about?

I had been helping. I had been respectful. I was doing everything. I was the only one.

The hurt crept in slow, like fog. But beneath it, something else stirred. I was getting older. I was beginning to see the shape of things I hadn't been able to name before.

And I realized:

My mother could never say anything good about me.

Not to others. Not even to herself.

She didn't want me to shine.

She didn't want me to see the good in others either.

Why? I still don't know.

But when someone is your only source of love, you don't question it.

You just keep trying to earn it.

I should've asked her why she said those things.

Why she told my sister I was cruel.

But I didn't.

I didn't want to make her uncomfortable.

I didn't want to seem ungrateful.

I was angry for five minutes.

Then the voice came back—Maybe I'm not doing enough. Maybe I am rude. Maybe I am all the things they say I am.

Maybe I've always been the problem.

Maybe that's why they sent me away.

That voice follows me still.

I didn't look forward to my sister's letters anymore. Sometimes, when she called, I'd find something else to do. Not because I stopped loving her—no. It was because when someone I trust, someone who gives me a fraction of safety, commits even the smallest betrayal, I pull away.

Because now I can't trust them.

My mother's tactics were systematic.

If people didn't pull away from me, eventually, I'd pull away from
them.
Like a game of chess.
And I was the pawn.
But why?
Why me?
Would knowing the answer make it better, or just bring more
questions?
Would it quiet the noise in my head?

Chapter 23: When I Let Myself Hope

I finally got a job.

A real job.

It was minimum wage, sure, but it was something I had earned all by myself. That made it everything. I was excited — not just for the paycheck, but for the chance to prove I could be something. I met new people, tried my best to be my best. I was a hard worker, almost too hard sometimes. My manager would even tell me, "You don't have to do everything, Isla."

Imagine that — someone noticing me. Someone telling me I could rest.

But I know now, I wasn't just trying to work hard. I was trying to be liked. To be seen. I wanted people to genuinely want me around. I went above and beyond — and then some — because part of me still believed that being liked had to be earned. That love was something you worked for.

Some of my coworkers saw that. Some took advantage. And honestly? I didn't mind. Not then. It was like I wore a sign on my chest that said, "Take advantage of me — I need to feel appreciated."

It wasn't admiration I was chasing. It was connection. Belonging. Worth.

And I can't blame them entirely.

They didn't know my story.

One day, while I was cleaning a table, a familiar voice called out.

"Isla? Is that you? Your name's Isla, right?"

I looked up. The face was a little older, but the smile was the same.

"Tony?" I asked.

"You know it!" he laughed.

Tony had been one of my closest friends through elementary and middle school. It had only been a few years, but it felt like a lifetime. We exchanged numbers and made plans to catch up. There was

nothing romantic — just a pure, joyful reconnection. And in that
moment, I felt it:
I was starting to build a life that belonged to me.
I left work that day with a bounce in my step. A small dream formed:
more friends, maybe a car, maybe... something better. When good
things happened, my mind ran wild — building futures I didn't think
I was allowed to have. But still, I let it run.
As I hopped on the bus heading home,
I accidentally gave myself hope.
Tony and I started talking more. We'd meet up here and there, mostly
after work or on a weekend afternoon. Nothing fancy — just walks,
long conversations, and laughter I hadn't heard in years, especially not
coming from my own mouth.
With him, I could let my guard down. There was no performance. No
proving. Just... me.
That was rare.
And I clung to it more tightly than I should have.
Because underneath all the light, I was still living in the shadow of my
home. That house never let you forget who you were supposed to be.
And no matter how good the outside world made me feel, I always had
to walk back through that door.
Sometimes, my mom would ask where I was going.
Sometimes she wouldn't.
But if she sensed joy in me — something independent from her — it
never ended well. Her comments would come sideways: a joke, a jab, a
sigh that somehow became my fault. She never said don't be happy,
but it was implied. Like there was only so much light to go around —
and I didn't deserve more than my share.
Tony started to notice.
"You okay?" he'd ask.
I'd smile. "Of course."
It's strange how easy it is to lie when the truth feels too big to explain.

I had no words for emotional abuse back then. No framework for manipulation or gaslighting. I just knew that whenever I felt too happy, too free, something would come along to pull me back down. And I let it. Because I didn't know I was allowed to push back.

One night, Tony picked me up after work.

We were supposed to grab something to eat — nothing fancy, just two old friends catching up. I always thought his jeep was the coolest thing. Riding around in it made me feel free, like maybe I belonged in a life where people looked forward to seeing me.

Before dinner, he said he needed to stop by his house. His mom was working late, and it would just be the two of us. I didn't think twice.

Not even once.

We walked into his room, and he was excited to show me his karaoke machine — something I'd only heard about at that time. He knew I loved music and singing, and this felt like a sweet gesture. We sat and listened to songs, and slowly, he moved closer. Then closer still.

He leaned in to kiss me.

I froze. Part of me didn't want to hurt his feelings. But the truth was, I didn't feel that way about him. I never had. Tony was my friend. My safe place. I wasn't scared of him — not then.

I pulled back with a laugh, trying to lighten the moment.

"Oh gosh, what are you doing?"

He smirked. "So it's like that?"

"Yeah," I said, still smiling a little. "It's like that."

And then something changed. In an instant.

His face twisted. Something in him snapped.

He grabbed my hair and yanked me down. One hand in my scalp, the other ripping at my shirt, undoing my pants. I fought. I fought with everything I had left. But he was faster. Stronger. Brutal.

Eventually, I shut down.

The fight left me.

I don't even know when. But I remember the moment I stopped feeling like a person.

When it was over, he threw my clothes at me.

"Get dressed," he said, like it was nothing. "I'll take you home."

And I went.

How strange is that? To be violated, brutalized, and then... offered a ride. I sat in his jeep, in silence, bleeding inside. I didn't run. I didn't scream. I didn't do anything.

We parked in front of my house. My lip had blood on it, dried and cracked. He took a napkin, spit on it, and gently dabbed it away.

"You got a little something there."

I didn't move.

Then he said, "Call me, okay? Maybe we can hang out again."

I just looked at him.

Not speaking. Not blinking.

Frozen.

I wanted to move. I wanted to run.

But maybe I was still waiting for permission.

As I got out of the Jeep, I stood frozen on the sidewalk in front of my house.

I must have stood there for what seemed like forever.

I knew I would get no comfort or support for what I had just experienced.

There would be no kind words spoken to me. No shelter for my pain.

So I just stood there—in my own head—trying to make sense of not only what happened, but what was to come.

A Letter to the Girl on the Sidewalk
You didn't deserve this.
Not the hands. Not the silence. Not the shame.
Not the weight you carried on trembling legs as you stood on that
sidewalk and stared at the door, knowing no one would open it with
love.
You weren't made to be abused.
You were made to feel things deeply.
To hope too hard.
To believe that even in a broken world, someone would be good to
you.
And when they weren't, it wasn't your fault.
Not because you missed the signs.
Not because you were too trusting.
Not because you smiled too wide or said yes to dinner or didn't run
fast enough.
It was never you.
They didn't hurt you because of who you were.
They hurt you because of who they were.
And the fact that you still cry — that you can still cry —
means you didn't lose your softness.
That is not weakness.
That is a miracle.
You didn't have a safe place to fall.

You didn't have arms to run into.
You had yourself, and somehow, that was barely enough.
But it was enough to get you here.
To this page.
To this moment.
To this life where your voice is no longer trapped behind your teeth.
So cry for her.
Hold her in your mind.
Tell her she didn't imagine it.
Tell her she didn't deserve it.
Tell her she is still here.
And that she will write her way into light.
Because that girl on the sidewalk?
She is not a victim.
She is the beginning of a warrior.

Chapter 24: A Secret I Swore I'd Keep

I couldn't tell anyone what had happened. Not even my mother. Something deep inside told me it wouldn't be safe. This may have been the first time I understood the truth about cause and effect in my world — I was the cause, and the effect was always pain. This was a secret I planned to carry to my grave.

But the universe has a way of exposing even our most hidden wounds. Not long after that night, I began to feel sick. Exhausted. My body betrayed me with fatigue I couldn't explain. I had always been full of energy, ready for whatever came next — but now, I could barely move. At first, my mom noticed in passing. Then her concern turned sharp. "What's going on with you?" she asked. "I hope you're not pregnant." That was the first time it even occurred to me — that it was possible. And with that thought, the weight of everything collapsed on top of me.

I went into my room, lay on my bed, and cried until I couldn't breathe. It had been almost a month of hiding my symptoms before my mother began demanding answers. The constant nausea. The exhaustion. The silence.

One afternoon, she sat next to me on the bed. Her voice was gentle. "Is there something you need to talk to me about?"

And I believed her. I believed she could hold my pain. I trusted, for one fragile moment, that maybe this time would be different.

So I told her.

I told her everything about that night. The jeep. The music. The shift from comfort to violation. I told her through tears and trembles, desperate for her to tell me I hadn't done anything wrong.

There was a long silence.

She rubbed my back and said, "Please. You're telling me you were a virgin?"

I blinked.

"Yes," I whispered. "I was."

Her face changed. She stood up and walked out of the room. I followed her, panic rising in my chest.

"I was a virgin before this!" I cried. "I wasn't promiscuous! I was a good girl!"

She didn't stop. "Mmhmm, I'm sure you were. That's why your uncles don't want you around their kids. They told me things and I always defended you. Now you do this to me?"

"You're probably pregnant now! But you had to have dick, didn't you? Now you're gonna call it rape?!"

I froze in the hallway. The air was too heavy to breathe.

"You don't get to walk away from this!" she screamed. "You teased him. You got what you wanted and now you're in trouble. And I have to fix it! I always have to fix what you fuck up!"

"You're such an embarrassment. You always have been."

I went back to my room and shut the door. Slowly. Quietly. I sat on the edge of my bed in silence.

Was it my fault? Did I send the wrong signal?

I could hear her in the other room, already on the phone with someone. "Well, listen to this now!" she said, like it was a joke. Like I was a punchline.

And I drifted off to sleep, no longer wanting to be part of anything at all.

That night, something broke in me. Not because of what had happened with Tony — that wound had already scarred over in silence. But because of what followed. Because when I finally reached out for love, I was handed blame.

Because the one person I needed to believe me chose to betray me.

Again.

Chapter 24: A Day I'll Never Forget

Days went by and I didn't know what I was going to do. I wanted guidance of some sort but just couldn't trust anyone enough to talk about it. Back then, I never realized that there were any resources out there for girls like me. I was young, and the person I am today feels as though I should've tried harder to find those resources. But I didn't. By now, I had spent most of my days locked away in my room. Letters from my sister came fewer and farther between. Although I didn't have the same excitement when I received them anymore, they were still a small escape. Just now, writing this, I realized that the joy I once had from my sister's letters was taken from me too. The happiness I felt running outside to check the mail was happiness I wasn't allowed to have. My mom wanted me to believe she was my only source of joy and pain. That she had the power to give and take both—sometimes at the same time.

The thoughts in my mind raced like a tornado. The central theme always seemed to come back to one thing: I was born. That was the problem. I was the reason my mom couldn't have a better life. So she made me pay for that fact every chance she got. Not with fists, but with carefully crafted emotional abuse—the kind that doesn't bruise the skin but corrodes the soul.

One day, my mom walked into my room and said, "Get dressed. We have an appointment."

An appointment? As usual, I didn't ask any questions. I didn't think I was allowed.

We left the house and soon arrived at a clinic.

"You're getting rid of this baby today," she said.

I just nodded. "Okay."

Sitting in the waiting room, she filled out all the required paperwork. I sat silently, crying. I was terrified. Embarrassed. Overwhelmed by emotions I didn't know how to name. She leaned over and said quietly, "Don't cry now. I bet you weren't crying when he was screwing you."

Her words didn't stop the tears.

She walked up to the receptionist, and I heard her say, "Okay. Okay. Thank you." Then she came back and handed me some bus money. "You didn't need me when you got into this situation. You sure as hell don't need me now."

And she left.

I wasn't surprised. In a way, I was relieved. Her absence gave me space to feel what I needed to feel without the constant battering of her words.

I placed my hand on my stomach. This child—conceived in violence—was still a part of me. I wondered how I could go through with it. But how could I not? What would I do? Where would we live? How could I protect them if I couldn't protect myself?

Then they called my name.

The room was cold. The table, hard. The doctor was doing a job. The nurse beside me held my hand. It was painful. I felt violated all over again.

"I did this to myself," I kept thinking. "I did this to myself."

They asked if someone was waiting for me. I lied and said yes. I knew if I told the truth, they wouldn't let me leave. I didn't want comfort. I wanted to disappear.

They gave me a little bag with supplies and I began my journey home. Two bus rides. In pain. Soaked through. When I got home, no one was there. I closed my door and fell into bed.

Sometime later, I woke up to my grandmother standing over me. I blinked hard, unsure if it was a nightmare. But it wasn't.

"You deserve everything you're feeling right now," she said.

Then she was gone.

I curled into myself and wished I wouldn't wake up again.

—-

When the Illusion Shatters
I was done. I was hurting—physically and emotionally—and I didn't
see an end to any of it. Somewhere in my heart, I was beginning to see
things more clearly. When the truth finally arrives, it doesn't whisper.
It crashes in like a wave you never saw coming.
And here's the truth: hurt doesn't always come from strangers.
Sometimes it comes from the people you trusted most. The people you
begged to love you.
I used to believe that family was supposed to love you. Nurture you.
Celebrate your joy and catch you when you fall. But when you realize
you've never had any of that, something in you changes.
You begin to see the manipulation. The betrayal. The lies you were fed
just to keep you quiet and loyal.
And the most painful part? Realizing that it wasn't love.
It was control dressed in affection.
Obligation dressed in tradition.
I thought I was strong for surviving it.
But now I know the real strength came from finally telling the truth.
From saying—out loud—that I didn't deserve any of it.
That I am not what happened to me.
That I am still here.
And that I am not done yet.

Chapter 26: What A Day

I don't really know what I was thinking. I moved through myself like a visitor, like I didn't fully belong inside my own skin. For as long as I could remember, I'd always felt too much. And yet during this time, I felt... nothing. Void. Alone. I could still put on a good face, but inside, I was always struggling with who I really was.

My dad eventually returned with my brother and sister. He got a place nearby and allowed them to stay with us. It should've been a gloriously happy time in my life. And in some ways, it was. But I don't think I ever truly found what was left of me. I never got back to the remnants. Life went on and on and on.

I dropped out of school in my twelfth-grade year. I just couldn't take the subtle emotional bullying from Tony's friends anymore. I was unraveling. Strength felt like a language I no longer understood. I felt broken, and I didn't see an end to how I was feeling.

Thoughts crashed through me like waves with no rhythm, only force. When I looked in the mirror, the reflection didn't show me—it echoed every cruel word I'd ever absorbed. I felt ugly. Worthless. I questioned my very existence.

—

Chapter 27: When Hope Becomes Quiet

"Even when I didn't speak of my past, it spoke through me. Every fear, every need, every retreat—it knew my name."

There comes a point in life when you stop asking, "Why me?" and start asking, "What now?"

That's where I found myself.

I wasn't healed. I wasn't even hopeful. I was worn thin—like silence had scraped its nails down my spirit, leaving me hollow and reactive.

The world didn't stop spinning just because I was lost. So I began again. Not with conviction, but with the trembling steps of someone waking from years of emotional sleep. Not toward a dream. Not toward a plan. Just forward.

It wasn't bravery. It was survival. And sometimes, that's enough.

Adulthood came quickly. With it came an unfamiliar kind of independence. I moved out as soon as I turned eighteen. Now, my mom couldn't center all her attention on me—which, oddly enough, felt like relief. She still wanted me to visit constantly, but I needed space. Even with the distance, she called every day. I listened as she spoke of other family members the way she once spoke of me. Her love came with conditions—compliance bought warmth; disagreement brought distance.

Somehow, despite everything I'd been through, I managed to shut the doors in my mind. I didn't dwell on my childhood traumas—or on him. I didn't revisit my grandmother's disdain, the rape, or the scattered emotional in-betweens. I don't know how my brain protected me like that, but it did—or at least, I thought it did.

What I didn't understand then was that the trauma didn't need remembering to be present. It had become me. I was the aftermath. I didn't have to relive the past—I was living proof of it. It showed up in my actions, in my fears, in my anxious thoughts. I was a mosaic of survival—trauma stitched into every part of me, hidden beneath a practiced smile. I didn't recognize it then. But now, I do.

There were so many moments during those years that hurt or confused me—moments when I dared to trust someone, only to be crushed by that hope. There wasn't a single breaking point—just a quiet erosion of trust, grain by grain, until nothing remained.

I look back sometimes and wonder

how I didn't reach that point sooner—how, after everything I had already endured, I still held on to even a thread of belief in people.

Maybe it was hope's last ember, flickering inside me, refusing to die—even when the world tried to smother it.

Because my heart... it wouldn't let me stop hoping.

But surviving isn't the same as living.

And hope—even the quiet kind—still asks for more.

It waits in the background, whispering, "There must be something after this."

I wasn't ready to believe it yet.

But I was still listening.

Chapter 28: A Fragile Flight

"Even a fragile bird knows when it must fly. Not because it is ready—but because staying means forgetting how."

There are moments in life that don't feel like chapters.

They feel like pauses. Like a long breath between storms.

That's what this time became for me.

Not peace, exactly—but a kind of stillness. A stretch of days that blurred together, where nothing dramatic happened, but nothing truly healed either.

I was going through the motions, keeping busy, making decisions, trying my best to move forward. But inside, I was holding my breath—waiting for something. Maybe for things to fall apart again.

It's strange how silence can be both comforting and terrifying. Because when you've lived a life shaped by chaos, stillness doesn't always feel safe.

Sometimes, it feels like the warning before the noise returns. Although I was independent, I had roommates. I was eighteen, and it felt like life was finally beginning. I worked, paid my share of the bills, and did my best to present a version of myself to the world—someone capable, someone likable, someone who belonged.

But inside, I carried another self.

There were always two versions of me. The one I offered to others—put-together, funny, agreeable. And the one no one saw—the girl quietly screaming beneath the surface. She was filled with fear of everyone and everything. She second-guessed every move, questioned every compliment, braced for disappointment before it even arrived. She reminded me, in a whisper that never stopped, what my place in the world was.

Not enough.

Not worthy.

Not real.

Even in the smallest moments—ordering food, laughing with a coworker, choosing what to wear—I felt like I was performing. Like I was standing just outside of my own skin, hoping no one could see the real me beneath it. I didn't know how to let people in. Not really. I had friends. I even had fun. But nothing ever felt safe. Relationships came with rules I couldn't quite grasp. I didn't know how to be loved without suspicion. Didn't know how to feel joy without bracing for loss. Every good thing came with a shadow. And I never fully stepped into the light.

At night, when the noise settled and I was alone in my room, the doubts were the loudest. I'd replay conversations. Re-analyze glances. Wonder if I'd said too much. Or not enough. I wanted to be seen—but only in ways I could control. I wanted to be held—but feared what closeness might uncover.

Trust wasn't just broken. It was foreign.

And yet, even in the heaviness, I kept going. I kept working. I kept laughing. I kept pretending. Because something in me still believed that if I could just do everything right—be good enough, kind enough, helpful enough—maybe someone would finally stay.

Someone would finally see me... and not leave.

Every day felt like a repetition of the one before—until it didn't. I had built what I thought were walls, but they were paper-thin, made more of hope than strength. They crumbled under the weight of even the smallest gust of fear.

Then I saw him—Tony.

It was just a glimpse, a passing moment. He didn't see me. But I saw him.

And in that second, every ounce of strength I had disappeared. My chest tightened. My stomach flipped. I couldn't breathe. I couldn't move. I was eleven steps back into that night.

So I did the only thing that made sense at the time.

I left.

No warning. No long goodbye. I packed what little I owned and disappeared out of state. I didn't see it as a choice—it was survival. I didn't tell anyone where I was going. I just ran.

Because staying meant living in fear of the next encounter. Because seeing him once had nearly shattered me. Because I knew—if I stayed—the girl underneath would take over. And I might not come back from that.

I found work again, made ends meet the best I could. It wasn't glamorous or easy, but it was mine. I held on tightly to that small sense of control—even if most nights, I came home and cried into my pillow, still hearing the echo of old voices in my head. Still feeling like two people: the one they saw, and the one who whispered, "Don't forget who you are."

But distance has a way of offering just enough quiet to hear yourself again.

And in the midst of surviving, I met him.

My first husband, Jonas.

He was charming in the way broken people often are—disarming, attentive, and easy to talk to. And maybe I wasn't ready. Maybe I was just looking for something solid to stand on. But when he said he saw me—really saw me—I wanted so badly to believe it. And so I did.

Chapter 29: When the Locks Begin to Rattle:

"Even sealed doors eventually remember what's behind them. Healing
doesn't mean forgetting, it means daring to unlock what we survived."
Some chapters don't start with thunder.
They begin in the quiet aftermath—
when you're no longer breaking, just bent,
when life doesn't hurt less, it just demands more of you.
That's where I was.
Not healed. Not whole.
But learning how to carry myself anyway.
There was no defining moment. No grand revelation.
Just a slow return to myself, breath by breath, decision by decision.
And though I still flinched at echoes from the past, I was beginning to
see
that I didn't have to live there anymore.
I could write new endings.
Even if the beginning still haunted me.

—-

Day to day living brought moments of calm, but sometimes—without
warning.
I'd have what I called "flashbulb memories." A sudden burst of a
moment I thought I had forgotten. They came with images,
sensations, emotions that didn't match the present but clung to me all
the same.
As the years passed, I never realized that I had rewritten much of my
past in my mind. My brain had found a way to survive by organizing
trauma into compartments—like rows of storage units. Each locked

with a memory I didn't want to touch. The door rolled down, latched, and sealed with the lie: "You're fine. It's gone now."

So when I met Jonas, I was a shell of who I could have been—but I was also more than I had been before. If that makes sense. There was growth, yes. But I still had triggers. I still carried pain. The difference was, I had convinced myself that everyone had these same triggers. That my upbringing was no different from anyone else's. That I was not unique, and so, all my shortcomings were mine to own.

I told myself I lacked confidence because I wasn't the right size. I was too fat. Too emotional. Too much.

The truth? I was told almost daily that I wasn't good enough.

I cried at commercials that depicted a father and daughter. I said it was because I missed my dad. But really—it was because I never had that bond to begin with.

When someone in authority spoke to me, I tensed inside. Even when I had done nothing wrong, I braced for verbal correction. I had trained myself to expect reprimand—even in safety.

That fear never left. And somewhere along the way, I learned to apologize for existing. I said sorry to strangers, to friends, to furniture I bumped into. Once, someone I was dating turned to his friend and said, "She apologizes for everything."

The friend asked, "What is she apologizing for?"

And without missing a beat, he said, "For being alive."

My mind raced constantly. Every interaction became an analysis. Every smile, every silence, every pause—it all meant something, I thought. And because my memories were locked away, I blamed myself. I thought I was just... flawed.

Jonas met the surface version of me. The girl who laughed at the right times. Who seemed unsure, maybe, but full of potential. He saw a young woman looking for her place in life.

He had no idea what was behind the locked doors.

We dated on and off for months before we moved in together. And, of course, my mother was never far behind—reminding me that not only was Jonas not good enough for me, but that I had ruined my life.
By "ruined," she meant that I had chosen to live my own life. That I had left her. That I had the audacity to move forward without her.
Her words still landed like tiny arrows. "Ungrateful." "Selfish." "Embarrassment."
I carried guilt just for living. Every good moment with Jonas came with a cloud of shame I couldn't explain. Not then.
Clarity, it turns out, comes with age.
And sometimes—only after the locks start to rattle.

Chapter 30: Before the Cracks Appeared

"We didn't know the past was still breathing beneath us. We only knew how to hold each other above the water."

Jonas and I became each other's safe harbor.

We didn't need anyone else. Neither of us had a strong circle of friends, and truthfully—we preferred it that way. It was just us against the world, and we liked it that way. We chose it. The world felt unpredictable, but with each other, we could breathe.

We were a young couple trying to make ends meet. We lived in a tiny studio apartment above a garage. He worked in construction. I worked at a local grocery store as a clerk. Our income was modest, but our bond felt strong. We didn't need much—we had each other.

Jonas didn't know the full extent of my past. Not because I didn't trust him, but because, by then, even I had locked so much of it away that it almost didn't feel real anymore. The only piece that surfaced often enough to mention was my strained relationship with my mother. It became the explanation for everything—the reason I was emotionally sensitive, the cause of my jealousy, the weight behind my need to be reassured and loved.

Our intimacy was inconsistent. Tender some days, distant others. He was young, filled with desire and expectation, and I was still trying to understand what closeness meant. Sometimes I showed up with passion. Other times, I disappeared beneath the touch. We didn't talk about that part much. We just navigated it—messy and quiet.

After three years together, we got married. We were twenty-one, too young to know how young we really were. But we felt strong, felt ready. We believed love was enough.

We thought we had outgrown our pasts. We thought we were building something new, something better. In a way, we were. But we had also rushed into it—wanting so badly to prove we were nothing like the people who raised us.

So we pressed fast-forward on our lives: married young, built our world fast. It only made sense to start a family. If love hadn't always made sense in our childhood homes, maybe we could create a new version of it. Maybe, with a baby, we could anchor ourselves to something pure and good.

We had no idea what would come next. Only that we were chasing something we never truly received.

Chapter 31: When Love Was Enough, Until It Wasn't

"Sometimes love isn't lost all at once. It fades in the quiet, splinters in the silences, and leaves without ever slamming the door."
So here we were—two children playing make-believe.
At least, that's what it feels like now. The older version of me wants to reach back through time, grab those two young people by the shoulders and shout, "Wait! You don't have to prove anything. You have time. Take it. Enjoy each other awhile."
But we didn't wait. We didn't know how. The only guidance we had came from the very people we were trying so hard not to become. So we dove headfirst into parenthood—reckless, hopeful, and utterly in love with the idea of building a better story.
Our daughter was born, and she was perfect. More than I could have ever imagined.
We couldn't spoil her with gifts or wealth, but what we lacked in material things, we made up for with time, presence, and adoration. She walked before her first birthday, babbled words into the air, and smiled with the kind of confidence only a deeply loved child could wear.
Strangers would stop us—just to confirm what we already knew. They'd compliment her beauty, her calm nature, her brightness. And we would beam with pride, as if her loveliness proved that we were doing it right.
We still lived far from family, and maybe that was a blessing. Our little world—just the three of us—felt safe, whole. He was a nurturing father, a focused partner, and laughter often echoed through our tiny home.
Even when something triggered one of us, it didn't hit as hard. We had her.

She softened the blows of memory and fear. In our happiness, we let our guard down.

Never let your guard down.

We named her Renata—a name that meant reborn. And that's exactly what she was. A fresh start. A symbol of what love could create when given room to breathe.

We were so enamored with her—and maybe with ourselves as parents—that we didn't question whether we were ready for more. Of course we were. We had proven we could do this.

But we were wrong.

Our second daughter's journey began differently. The pregnancy was filled with complications. From the very start, there were signs. Warnings. Fear.

She was born six months early, fragile and fighting for her life. She had many health issues—some known, others still unfolding. Once she grew strong enough to travel, I felt pulled home. I needed my family nearby.

We were still clinging to that happiness. Still believing it could carry us through anything. We thought that maybe—now that we'd survived so much—we were stronger. That we could plant our roots anywhere, as long as we were together.

But the next few years would prove us wrong.

They would become the hardest years of our adult lives—not just as a couple, but as parents, and as children of people who were broken in ways we were only beginning to understand.

Chapter 32: The Shifting Ground

"Not all breaking sounds like shattering. Sometimes, it's the quiet erosion beneath your feet—the slow undoing of everything you thought was solid."

We thought we were strong enough. We had survived long nights in the NICU, whispered promises in sterile rooms, and watched a life we barely knew fight harder than most adults ever have to. That kind of battle changes you. It tightens your grip, sharpens your perspective. But it also wears you down. And somewhere between hospital visits and hopeful prayers, between exhaustion and fear, something began to change in us. Not all at once. Not loud. Just subtle shifts like ground quietly giving way beneath a house built too fast. Our love was still there, but it began to ache under the weight of everything we didn't know how to carry.

It's crazy to know that I wanted my family around during this time. Although they had proven to me, time and time again, that they could never be there for me during the moments I truly needed them, I still yearned for it. The fear of losing my baby was more than I could bear. My heart had already put away so many of the past disappointments, tucked them into quiet corners just to keep going. But now, facing this challenge, that deep, human need for connection took over. So we made the move to be near my family. His family wasn't an option. No one on his side had any stability. My mom had made a home for her and my brother and sister in New Mexico—and that's where we went. We packed up our two little ones and whatever we could fit in our car, and headed toward what we thought would be a better life. I don't know why I believed that at the time. Looking back, it makes no sense at all. I've always been confused about my feelings towards people, especially the ones in my immediate circle.

We named our youngest daughter Brielle, which means strength. We didn't realize the meaning at the time. But the name suited her well.

The drive to New Mexico was long, but we were fueled by something fragile, hope, maybe. Or desperation dressed up as purpose. We told ourselves this would be good. A fresh start. A chance to be close to people who were supposed to care, and wanted to help. But somewhere deep down, a part of me already knew what we were walking into.

Still, we arrived. My mom welcomed us in her own way, briefly warm, quickly critical. She had made a home for herself, my brother, and sister. We were simply guests in it. At first, everything was manageable. Brielle was growing stronger every day, her spirit quiet but fierce. She didn't cry much. She never demanded more than what we had to give. And somehow, even in her fragile body, there was a strength that made people pause. Renata, now a toddler, adjusted quickly. She was bright, curious, full of chatter and affection. Watching her care for her baby sister in her own little ways made my heart swell and ache at the same time.

I wanted to believe we were going to be okay. But the pressure of living under someone else's roof began to build. The things we couldn't say grew louder than the things we could. And just like that, the cracks that had formed between us, me and him, me and my mother, me and myself, began to widen. Brielle's name meant strength. We hadn't known that when we named her. But it fit her perfectly. And looking back, maybe I was the one who needed that reminder most.

Chapter 33: The Door That Closed Behind Us

"Sometimes the hardest part isn't walking away—it's knowing you were never meant to stay."

Brielle was a mystery from the beginning. She entered the world weighing just two pounds, wrapped in wires and quiet prayers. The doctors hadn't expected her to survive—yet there she was. Fragile, yes. But fighting. Her tiny body relied on oxygen and a feeding tube, and her strength came in soft, stubborn pulses. She didn't cry much. She simply endured. By the time she was strong enough to travel, we packed up everything we could fit into our car and made the move to New Mexico.

My mom had a three-bedroom apartment there. She gave us one of the rooms. My brother and sister shared the other. It was supposed to be temporary—just until we could find our footing. And at first, it worked. My mom wasn't loving toward my girls, but she wasn't unkind either—and that, to me, felt like a win. I had carried quiet hopes of her being a doting grandmother, but I let those go. We didn't need that from her. Jonas and I had enough love to carry our daughters forward.

He found a job quickly, and for a while, things looked hopeful. We paid the bills to lighten my mom's load, wanting to contribute, to show gratitude. Then the car broke down, and money—already stretched—snapped tight. Jonas bought a bicycle and rode to work each day. I handled Brielle's appointments, her equipment, the buses, the stares. I carried her oxygen, pushed the stroller, held Renata's hand.

It was hard—but she was safe. That was all that mattered.

When Jonas was at work, the mother I remembered—the one who found fault in anything that made me happy—would resurface. She made snide comments about Jonas's soft-spoken nature, questioned his manhood, and planted dark seeds about his bond with Renata. I knew what she was doing. She'd always tried to dismantle the pieces of joy I built for myself. And yet, we stayed—because there was nowhere else to go.

Until the day we came home from another of Brielle's appointments, and my mom met us at the door in a panic. "The apartment owners found out you all are staying here. They're going to kick me out!" She was frantic. Worried. And I understood. She had my brother and sister to think about. I felt terrible, like my little family had become a burden she never asked for.

Jonas had just paid the rent and utilities, so we had nothing left for a place of our own. Still, I tried to fix it. I called a shelter. They could take us, but not for a week. A clean place, they promised. With a kitchenette. A chance to get on our feet. One more week. But when I told her, she didn't even pause. "No, no. That's not going to work, Isla," she said. "You all need to go now. Today." So, without hesitation. We packed our little family up, and went into a temporary shelter. We had no money, no car and although we were grateful to have a place to go at all, we felt lost. We came to find out later, that the apartment manager knew about us the entire time we were there, and she didn't tell my mom that we had to leave. My mom wanted us to leave, and she couldn't wait another week.

The Weight I Still Carry

As I sit here now, my Brielle is asleep in her room. The machines hum and hiss around her, expanding her lungs, feeding her breath. I've grown used to the sound. It's part of the rhythm of our life, loud, constant, necessary.

The memory I just wrote used to fill me with only sadness. Today, there's still sadness, but also anger. So much anger.

This process, writing this memoir, has made me reflect in ways I never could've imagined. I started this to help others like me. People who ask themselves, *Why am I like this?* People who wonder why they're always waiting for the ground to shift. Why their hearts race in silence. Why they flinch at kindness. Why they trust no one, not even themselves.

Every decision I've ever made has been a direct reflection of what was done to me. Every choice shaped by survival. Every fear inherited from wounds I never asked for.

And sometimes, I get a glimpse of the person I might have been. Who I was "meant" to be, before all of it.

There are times I cry for no reason. At least, that's how it seems. To others. Even to myself, sometimes. The grief is quiet but constant. It rises up in the middle of the ordinary, like folding laundry, watching TV, driving in silence,and crashes without warning.

My heart aches without explanation.

—-

Chapter 34: When Love Isn't Enough

"We tried to love each other through the wounds we never named.
But love, without healing, becomes a lifeline that frays in silence."
After the shelter, we moved again, hoping that distance might bring
peace. Hoping we could find our way back to what Jonas and I once
had.

I told myself it was just us now. That we could only count on each
other. And in many ways, that was true. Especially when it came to
Brielle. Her health was fragile and demanding. No daycare could safely
support her, so I stayed home and became her full-time caregiver.
Eventually, we had our third daughter. Her name is Zara.
She arrived like a burst of sunlight, vibrant, loud, impossibly alive. She
filled the cracks in our world with laughter and chaos and a kind of
fearless joy that reminded me how to breathe again.
And through it all, there was Renata.
She had already seen more than most children her age. And still, she
never complained. We tried to protect her from the weight we carried,
but she was always watching. Always absorbing.
She was a beautiful big sister, gentle with Brielle, patient with Zara,
endlessly willing to help. Even when she went without—without toys,
without attention, without answers—she met it all with quiet grace.
There was a strength in her that I didn't yet have the words to name.
But over time, Jonas and I began to drift.
Not loudly. Not all at once.
The cracks were quiet at first. But they widened, slowly, until they
became part of the landscape between us. I blamed myself. I had
convinced myself he was all I needed—my everything, outside of our
children. And when someone becomes your everything, fear creeps in.
Fear of losing them. Fear of not being enough.

That fear turned into neediness. Possessiveness. I was jealous of anyone who got his attention. I didn't see it then, but I was already driving a wedge between us.

When he reconnected with his family, I should've been happy. But I wasn't. I felt left behind. I wanted to be the only one who mattered.

But that wasn't love—that was fear disguised as devotion. That was trauma, clinging to the illusion of safety.

Still, he was a good father.

Afraid, yes—especially of Brielle's medical needs—but he loved her. He showed up. He tried. We both did.

And now, with distance, I can finally see the truth:

We had been each other's rescue, once. But we hadn't healed. We had never made space for it. Not after our childhoods. Not after Brielle.

There was no room to pause or reflect—only to survive.

And you can't build a forever on survival.

We were good parents. But we weren't good for each other.

Eventually, he met someone who could give him what I couldn't. And maybe that's what he needed.

At the time, I didn't think anything was wrong with me. I thought I was doing what I had promised myself I would always do:

Be the best mother you can be. No matter what.

And for a while, I did.

Until someone came into my life who would force every buried trigger to the surface.

—-

Chapter 35: The Shape of Familiar Things

When Jonas and I divorced—or rather, before the divorce was even final—I dove straight into another relationship.
I didn't want to be alone.
I couldn't be alone.
What I needed was healing.
What I reached for was distraction.
But when you don't even know there's a wound, what are you seeking healing for?
I told myself the story I needed to survive: that it was all him, not me. That I had been the one left behind. That I deserved this new beginning. And maybe part of that was true. But another part—the louder part—was rooted in something I couldn't yet name.
My memory was still compartmentalized. Locked away.
Each compartment held a version of me—quiet, fractured, unfinished.
Every traumatic piece I'd buried was still creating the woman I had become.
And I didn't even know it.
I didn't stop to think about how fast I was moving on.
I didn't ask myself what my daughters needed, how they might feel about someone new.
I didn't really get to know him.
Not the real him.
Before I could see straight, I was already in love. Or what I thought was love.
James was strong.
He was handsome.
He was bad—but then suddenly, heartbreakingly good.
He was chaos.

And I was used to chaos.

In some twisted, unconscious way, I felt like this was where I belonged.

I knew how to function in dysfunction.

I had been trained in it.

And in that moment, familiarity felt safer than peace.

I didn't know why then.

But now—I do.

I would love to say the beginning of that relationship was wonderful.

Romantic.

An epic love story.

But it wasn't.

In less than a month, he was living with us.

My girls were still so little. Their world was small, and their biggest concern was where Mommy was. As long as I was near, they seemed okay. Or maybe that's just what I wanted to believe.

Within the first two months, James had already left us three times.

Each time, he packed his things and told me it was over.

Each time, he walked out, met someone else, stayed out until he was done.

And then he'd ask to come back.

And each time—I let him.

That's when something old started to stir inside me.

The compartments I had locked so tightly began to crack open.

Something buried was rising. A feeling I couldn't quite name yet. But it felt like being swallowed whole.

I didn't understand it at the time.

I just knew it didn't feel good.

I felt weak.

And I hated myself for it.

Here I was—raising daughters—while letting someone treat me like I didn't matter.

Was I showing them what love looked like? Or was I showing them
how to disappear?
I only wanted them to be strong. But I was anything but.
And still—I stayed.
Somehow, I convinced myself that strength meant not giving up.
That staying meant fighting for love.
That being chosen—even after being discarded—was proof that I
mattered.
But the truth was, I was terrified.
Terrified of being alone.
Terrified of not being chosen.
Terrified of what it might mean to face myself in the silence.
And then he came back again.
He chose me.
He was choosing me.
That's what I told myself as another compartment creaked open just a
little bit wider.
What came next?
Marriage.
Because marriage makes it all better, right?
That's what I told myself.
This would be the thing that finally changed everything.
We'd stop the cycle. We'd become a family.
Marriage meant commitment. Stability. Healing.
I had learned so much from my first marriage—or so I thought.
We were young, Jonas and I. Too immature. Too different.
He wasn't the man I needed.
He didn't know how to love me the way I needed to be loved.
That's what I believed.
And eventually, my brain decided my mother had been right all along.
She used to tell me, "You don't even know what a real man is."
Well—now I had a real man.

A man who got angry.
A man who made me feel small.
A man who called my name in a voice that felt more like thunder than tenderness.
Was this what a "real man" did?
Somewhere deep inside me, a voice answered: Yes.
And I hate that I believed it.
I hate that it felt familiar.
That I could settle so easily into pain as if it were an old coat.
That I wore disrespect like it was woven into the fabric of love.
Why?
Why did I convince myself that I deserved this?
I still don't know the full answer. But I know this:
Familiarity feels safe when chaos is all you've ever known.

The Voice I Didn't Know Was Mine
This memoir isn't about the ins and outs of every relationship I've had.
It's about the why behind the choices.
The feelings I didn't have names for—until now.
For most of my adult life, I've felt different from every other woman I met.
Not better. Not worse. Just... different. Like there was something wrong with me that I couldn't quite identify, but always felt gnawing at the back of my mind.

I didn't realize it then, but that feeling was a record that had been playing in the background all along.
Telling me I wasn't enough.
Telling me I was broken.
Telling me that any good thing would eventually leave—and that if something bad happened, it was probably my fault.
I didn't trust anyone.
And instead of recognizing that as a symptom of what I'd been through, I saw it as a flaw in who I was.
I never held people accountable for the ways they hurt me.
But I never gave myself grace, either.
I used to hear about people having nervous breakdowns, and I didn't understand.
I'd think, How could someone let themselves get that far gone?
But I never stopped to take a look at myself.
I never asked the hard questions.
I just existed in a world that taught me, again and again, that the hurt, the pain, the confusion—was my fault.
I believed I was the common denominator.
The problem.
And when I went out in public, I carried that belief with me like a scarlet letter.
I just knew that everyone could see it.
That somehow, I wore the label on my chest:
"This one is different. This one is broken."

Chapter 36: The Echo of Familiar Things

By now, I had lived away from my mother and grandmother for years.
And yet—looking back—I see that they never really left.
That's the thing about trauma.
It follows you.
It lingers in your choices, in your silence, in the shape of your relationships.
It echoes inside the parts of you that never learned how to breathe without bracing.
That's the kind of scar toxic parents leave behind.
They don't always raise broken children.
Sometimes, they raise adults who spend their entire lives trying to make sense of nonsense.
After a year of dating James, we got married.
The red flags weren't hidden.
They were waving. Loud. Obvious.
His temper. His drinking. His infidelities.
I ignored them all.
In fact—if I'm honest—sometimes I looked forward to our fights.
Because after the fighting came the apology.
The softness. The tenderness.
The moment where I felt seen.
No one had ever been apologetic to me before.
Not like that.
And in some twisted way, the apology became more meaningful than the betrayal itself.
That's what trauma does.
In the beginning, intimacy came easily with James.
He was handsome—built like a god. And he wanted me.
That alone felt like a victory. Like a long-awaited validation.
He wasn't gentle like Jonas.

He was familiar.

Familiar in a way I thought I had buried.

Familiar in the way chaos can feel like home when it's the only thing you've ever known.

I didn't understand why it felt so right, even with all the wrong.

I had never experienced pleasure like that before—not in that part of my relationships.

So I told myself: This is what normal must feel like.

And I clung to it.

But trauma has a way of sneaking back in when you least expect it.

The moment he confessed to sleeping with someone else—something in me broke.

Not just my heart.

Something deeper. Older.

The voices came back.

The same old rhetoric. The same shame.

But this time, they were louder.

I hadn't heard them in so long, I thought maybe they were gone.

But they weren't. They were just waiting.

Suddenly, I couldn't stand the way he touched me.

I cringed. I pulled away.

I told myself he didn't want me.

That maybe he never did.

That maybe he was just in love with the idea of me—

The broken girl with a beautiful face.

The wounded one who made him feel like a savior.

He was the bad boy who wanted to be better.

But he was still battling his own demons.

And I...

I had never stopped battling mine.

The years crept on slowly—one fragile thread at a time.

Our marriage became a cycle of breakups and makeups.

Love, anger, apology, repeat.
We moved so often that I spent more time unpacking boxes than building a life.
One minute he wanted us.
The next, he wanted us as far away from him as possible.
And the sad part? I waited.
Waited to see what he wanted to do with my life.
Boxes. I hated boxes.
I hated the packing. The unpacking. The never-ending transition.
We never stayed long enough for roots.
I never stayed long enough for peace.
I had spent my childhood searching for a place to belong.
Now, I was searching for a place to call ours.
Something stable. Something real. Something safe.
I was a loving and devoted mother to my girls.
But I was careless with their childhood.
Jonas had moved on. He was in a stable and loving relationship.
He wanted custody of the girls. Well—two of them.
Brielle, he said, was too much for them to handle.
That responsibility had become mine alone.
But I couldn't give the others up.
I couldn't.
I told myself they weren't suffering.
That the constant moves were an adventure.
That changing schools wasn't a big deal.
That as long as I was there, they would never feel abandoned.
So they stayed.
With me. Through all of it.
Through the fights.
Through the tears.
Through bottles being thrown and things breaking.
Through the sound of their mother breaking, over and over again.

I failed at the one thing I had sworn I would get right:
Being a good mother.
They were never neglected.
Never physically harmed.
But they were emotionally bruised by the life I allowed around them.
And I didn't even see it.
Not until it was too late.
When James drank—or got angry—it made all of us nervous.
We walked on eggshells, always watching for signs.
I did my best to shield my girls from him during those moments.
But when he was good... he was really good.
He was great with them.
And he adored Brielle.
More than anyone else, he stepped in where Jonas never could.
He understood Brielle's limitations.
He saw her. He was gentle with her.
He made time for all of us—little family outings, games, cooking
meals.
Moments that mattered. Especially to me.
Because for Brielle, the world was already so limited.
And when someone entered her world with kindness, it felt like a
miracle.
That alone made me want to endure everything else.
I saw the good in him.
And I didn't want to lose that.
I know it might not make sense—but at the time, it made all the sense
in the world to me.
Because I didn't know if I'd ever find that again.
And the truth is—I didn't even know what "normal" looked like.
How could I?
No one had ever shown me.
I had no friends.

No one to ask for advice.
It was just me—making decisions for all of us.
I told myself: Renata and Zara had their dad.
But Brielle? She needed someone like James.
And maybe...I needed someone like James, too.
Because I was starting to wear down.
The kind of tired that sleep can't fix.
I was overwhelmed and I didn't know why.
Just that life felt heavier than I could carry.
So I made a decision—maybe not out loud, but deep down:
Take whatever life throws at you. Just survive it.
Because I was tired.
And when you're that tired, sometimes enduring feels easier than escaping.

Chapter 37: What Love Was Supposed to Be

I didn't know how far gone I was until I stopped recognizing my own reflection.

Not in the mirror, but in the way my girls looked at me.

In the way I'd stopped laughing.

In the way I spoke to myself when no one was listening.

I had spent so long trying to hold everything together that I hadn't noticed the cracks weren't just in the walls around me—they were in me.

The truth is, I had started to disappear.

Not all at once.

But in pieces. Quietly.

In every apology I made for him.

In every excuse I told the girls.

In every time I told myself, this is just how life is.

That's what happens when you confuse endurance with love.

When you think that staying means strength.

When you've never seen what love is supposed to be.

James didn't hurt me every day.

Some days were good.

Some days, he was everything I wanted him to be.

And those were the days I lived for.

The days that gave me just enough hope to silence the rest.

Because when you've grown up in chaos, a calm day feels like a promise.

Even if it's just a pause between storms.

I kept telling myself he loved me.

That his anger came from pain.

That I could fix him.

That I was the right kind of broken for him to heal beside.
But what I didn't see—what I couldn't admit—was that I was slipping away.
And my daughters were watching.
Through the years, our pattern never really changed.
The girls and I would move away. Or he would leave.
Then somehow, we'd always find our way back to each other.
Each time came with a new promise, a new vow.
We'll do better. We'll be better.
But nothing ever really changed.
And the whole time, the background noise in my head never stopped.
The voices of failure. Of shame. Of self-doubt.
Every time he got angry, every time I made another excuse—I lost a piece of myself.
What I didn't realize was that there wasn't much of me left to lose.
Then—my mother moved into the mother-in-law suite beside us.
It was the worst thing that could've happened.
I hadn't lived near her in years. And with the old compartments of memory cracking open again, it was only a matter of time before everything I had tried to hold back came rushing in.
It started small. Little things.
I'd come home to hear her whispering accusations—
Telling me that Zara and Renata had boys over.
Painting them as rebellious. As disrespectful. As wild.
Then I'd hear the other side.
Zara and Renata telling me their own grandmother was calling them names.
Cruel names.
Names no child should ever hear from someone who's supposed to love them.
That's when something in me snapped.
Not in anger. Not in rage.

But in clarity.
This was my line.
My girls were, and are, my world.
And no one, not even my mother, was going to poison that.
For the first time in a long time, I took control of something.
I told her she had to leave.
And even in that, I gave her more grace than she ever gave us.
I told her she had until the end of the month.
With clarity and power came something else.
Bitterness.
Resentment.
Jonas, having seen the toll of the verbal abuse, decided he wanted Zara and Renata for the entire summer—not just on weekends. He wanted to give them peace.
I didn't fight him.
Brielle stayed with me, and I was okay with that.
She was enrolled in a day program, and either James or I could be home when she returned.
My mom had gathered the rest of her things and left.
Without her there, the air felt different—lighter.
It was a hundred degrees less stressful.
I felt like I could take on the world.
I actually thought: Nothing can stop me now.
Until something did.
That afternoon, I pulled into the
driveway just in time to meet Brielle's bus.
We walked into the house like any other day.
She went to her room, and I helped her out of her school clothes.
She sat at her little desk, happily working on her crafts—oblivious to the storm forming around us.
And that's when I felt it.
The house felt wrong.

Still. Empty.

Like something had been removed—but not just things. Presence.

I went to put my things away.

And then I saw it.

In the bedroom—his things were gone.

Not a few items. Not a drawer.

Gone.

I opened the closet.

Empty.

Checked the drawers.

Nothing.

My breath caught in my chest.

I ran to the garage.

Tools,gone. Bags, gone. He was gone.

I couldn't wrap my mind around it.

We hadn't been fighting.

I thought things were fine.

I thought we were in a good place.

No.

He wouldn't just leave.

Not without a word. Not without a call.

He would've told me. He had to have told me.

I ran back inside.

Opened the closet again like maybe I was wrong.

Like maybe I had imagined all of this.

But I hadn't.

He was gone.

No note. No text. No goodbye.

And I collapsed on the living room floor.

Just sank.

Not into anger.

Not even grief.

Just absence.
And the only thought that came to me, from somewhere deep and
buried and aching was:
"My poor dad."

Chapter 38: After the Echo

Although we were married, James and I shared nothing that truly bound us—no children together, no joined finances I couldn't untangle. It meant he could vanish whenever he pleased. He had no tangible obligation to me.

Technically, I could survive on my own. The money would be tight but possible. What I didn't want was to be alone—again. And I had no one to turn to for comfort or counsel. Every time I imagined reaching out, I pictured the verdict: This is your fault.

Renata and Zara wouldn't be surprised; departures had become routine for them. But this time felt different. I kept replaying the last few weeks—no arguments, no tension—our best stretch in years. And then one silent exit. A blindsiding.

Thoughts of Micah rushed over me—how he must have felt believing life was finally coming together, only to meet a different reality. I was drowning in that same confusion.

I felt lost, scared, abandoned, alone, and ashamed. Something in me wanted to curl into the smallest space and disappear from the world, convinced it would be better for everyone.

But I had Brielle.

I took a few days off work and told no one what had happened. No calls, no texts—certainly not to James or his family. I wouldn't beg anyone to love me.

Something broke during those days. Not a clean snap—more like a spreading fracture that became physical. My body ached everywhere. Flashes of half-memories blinked behind my eyes, freezing me mid-step. I felt I was losing my mind.

Late the third afternoon, the pressure inside me became unbearable. I led Brielle to the living room, sat her on the floor, and poured out a bottle of pills. "Brielle," I whispered, "you and Mommy are going to sleep, okay?"

Pure trust filled her face. She smiled. "Sleep, Mommy?"

"Yes, baby—sleep."

Because in that moment I believed the world, and Brielle's world, would be kinder without us.

She stood, wrapped her arms around my shoulders and said, "It's okay, Mommy. We can sleep now." Then she carefully handed me what she thought were my pills, took a handful for herself, and said, "Mine."

That trust—so innocent, so complete—traveled through me like lightning. I felt her love in my bones.

I gathered every pill, swept them into my palm, and tossed them into the trash. Brielle gasped: "Mommy! Sleep?"

I pulled her close. "I'm not tired anymore, Brielle."

And I wasn't. Her love pulled me back from the edge.

I had been searching for unconditional love in a man who could never give it, while the truest love I'd ever known was sitting right beside me. My children had been that love all along.

That night, after putting Brielle to bed, I sat in the dark and felt utter disgust at what I'd almost done. But beneath the disgust was understanding: I hadn't merely broken that night—I had shattered. Years of hidden fractures finally gave way.

My mind had tried to protect me by burying memories, but forgetting pain only made me think I was crazy. I wasn't. I was wounded—again and again—until the wounded places themselves split open. And in the splitting, everything demanded to be faced.

I was shattered. But shattered pieces can be gathered—slowly, painfully—and forged into something stronger than before.

I'm sharing these moments because they were the fault lines of my life—places where everything shifted. Trauma doesn't look the same for everyone, but it always changes who we were meant to be. For years I thought there was something wrong with me because I wasn't "as strong" as other women who survived similar hurt. Only when I searched myself did I find the truth: my mind had been trying to protect me. It sealed memories behind locked compartments so I could keep going, but that same protection kept me from understanding my pain—let alone acknowledging it. Naming the hurt doesn't make it vanish, but it takes away its power to define me in silence. That's why I'm telling it now.

Chapter 39: The First Small Steps

The morning after I threw the pills away, sunlight slipped through the blinds as if night hadn't tried to swallow us whole. Brielle padded into the kitchen wearing mismatched socks and the brightest grin—utterly unaware that her love had kept us both here.
I brewed coffee and felt an unsettling calm, like the hush after a storm when you're not sure which trees will keep standing.
"What now?"
I'd asked that question for other people—how to soothe James's anger, how to shield my girls—but never for "me". This time it lingered for days, humming until it turned into a clear answer:
"You need help. Real help. Find a therapist."

—-

A Single Call
Jonas answered on the second ring.
"James is gone," I said.
He wasn't surprised, but he didn't judge. When he offered to bring Zara and Renata home early, I asked him not to. "Let their summer be their summer," I said. "I'll handle it when they're home."

—-

Quiet Summer
When the girls called, we laughed about campfires and sand-dune adventures. I told them Brielle and I were fine—and somehow, we were. Nights were quiet. Mornings began with oatmeal smiles.

—-

Finding Dr. Shivaro

I scanned therapist lists, waited on hold, and almost gave up—until Dr. Shivaro answered her own phone, calm and direct. Her first opening was Thursday at 3 p.m. I wrote it on a sticky note and pressed it to the fridge like a lifeline.

First Session

I walked in hoping she could fix me in one hour, already certain she'd decide I was a joke. We sat. She asked, "Why now?"

Everything poured out: failures I could name, fears I'd never voiced, the pills on the table. The deeper memories stayed locked, but the weight I could reach finally had a voice. She barely spoke—just listened, steady as a shoreline.

When the hour was up she closed her notebook and said, "There is nothing wrong with you, Isla. You need to know that."

Tears I hadn't planned slipped free. No one had ever said the flaw wasn't me.

She handed me a tissue, booked the next appointment, and sent me into late-afternoon sun with those words echoing in my chest.

That night I repeated the promise I'd begun whispering: *One more sunrise. One honest step. Repeat.*

—-

Summer's End

Summer slipped away. Zara and Renata came home sun-kissed and laughing. Over dinner I told them simply, "James decided to leave." I spared them the image of empty closets. Brielle and I carried that alone.

Life pressed forward: school schedules, clock-in hours, bus pickups, bills on the fridge.

What I looked forward to most was Thursday afternoons with Dr. Shivaro.

—-

Homework of Healing
At the end of our second session she slid a card across the table:
Answer honestly each night:
1. Do you constantly seek approval?
2. Do you fail to recognize your own accomplishments?
3. Do you fear criticism?
4. Do you overextend yourself?
5. Do you need perfection?
6. Are you uneasy when life is going smoothly?
7. Do you feel responsible for others?
That evening, after the girls slept, I opened a fresh notebook and wrote
without censoring:
1. Absolutely.
2. What accomplishments?
3. Yes—criticism equals failure.
4. Maybe. Probably.
5. I demand it of myself.
6. Very. Good never lasts.
7. Always.
It looked less like homework and more like an X-ray—showing bones
of
belief I'd carried so long I mistook them for truth.
The next Thursday I slid the notebook toward her. She read silently,
then said, "This is a beginning, not an indictment. We'll work on
every line."
For the first time since James left, I felt hope—not the fragile hope
that someone would stay, but the sturdier hope that "I" might.
I walked to the car whispering the mantra again: *One more sunrise.
One honest step. Repeat*

Chapter 40: Familiar Echoes

Months slipped by, marked not by crisis but by Thursday afternoons in Dr. Shivaro's lavender office. My spiral notebook thickened with nightly answers, and distance settled gently between me and my family. Mom moved in with my sister; I stopped pressing for weekly visits. For the first time, that boundary felt like medicine, not rebellion.

Life grew quieter in ways I hadn't known to want—until the afternoon James knocked on the door.

I let him in. Relief rose first: maybe I wouldn't have to carry every decision alone. Therapy lessons fluttered but the feeling that settled was the oldest one—familiar. I brewed coffee for two, convincing myself I was demonstrating growth by giving him another chance. In truth I was mistaking predictable chaos for safety.

—-

Reflection — Familiar as a Compass

I'm writing this moment because it exposes the circuitry trauma builds in a survivor's mind. Even with therapy insight, my first instinct was still to choose familiar—because familiar pretends to be safe. Trauma rewires the compass: predictable pain feels less frightening than unpredictable peace. If your pattern looks different—substances, self-harm, a job you hate—

know the wiring can change, but first it has to be seen. I'm writing this so you can see my wiring and maybe recognize a sketch of your own.

I used to tell myself I simply wanted a "real family." I imagined real looked like dinners where everyone stayed, laughter that didn't end in slammed doors, a house where love felt solid. So every time James left and returned, I convinced myself I was trying—trying to make us real, trying to prove I wasn't the girl who always got abandoned.

Therapy was teaching me language, but the trauma still shaped my logic in ways I couldn't yet see. I kept thinking the problem lived in James's temper, his drinking, his disappearances. Fix him, and we'd be fine.

But the unseen compartments inside me had already sculpted my decisions:

- Insecurity disguised as devotion
- Control mistaken for safety
- Neediness painted as unconditional love

James wasn't the enemy; he was the mirror reflecting my unhealed fractures. I walked into that relationship shattered, and a shattered heart makes choices a healthy mind would never consider logical. Looking inward hurt, because the answers didn't flatter me. They whispered:

It isn't about proving you're lovable; it's about believing you are, even alone.

It isn't about controlling chaos; it's about unclenching your fists long enough to see if calm can hold you.

And healing won't arrive through someone else's apology—it begins the moment you admit you're broken and still worthy of being pieced together.

These weren't the answers I wanted.

But they were the answers I needed.

—-

Missing Thursday

Family drama swept in before I could answer the first warning signs. Group texts twisted into accusations and silences. To prove I was still "family material," I hosted Sunday dinner—lasagna, extra garlic bread, bottomless wine. We laughed too loud and numbed the rest. The therapist's card stayed on the fridge; crisis felt louder than healing.

That night, amid dirty glasses, I whispered, Next Thursday. One more sunrise. One honest step. Repeat.

—-

Years in Half-Light

Next Thursday turned into many. James's presence waxed and waned; my sessions thinned, then stopped. Hot-and-cold became the rhythm with my siblings—never cruel, never honest. Conversation skimmed safe surfaces; deeper truths stayed locked away.

I told myself I was strong for never missing an IEP meeting, for feeding everyone who knocked. But my daughters saw a mother who handed her worth to a man and her silence to a family that preferred small talk to truth.

I hadn't chosen myself over the cycle; I was still that scared little girl waiting for permission—only now inside a woman's life.

Perhaps my siblings will never know my version of the past, and I will never know theirs. Healing isn't a single choice—it's a promise you fail and try again until, one day, you keep it long enough for a new pattern to form.

Tonight I open a fresh notebook and write one line across the top: The pattern is familiar; the fight is new.

I underline it twice, set the pen down, and trust tomorrow to give me one more chance to choose differently.

I never missed a parent-teacher conference, never let a prescription run out, never skipped an IEP meeting for Brielle. I told myself that was strength—that as long as my girls felt supported, I was winning the fight against my past.

But children don't measure strength by calendars and checklists; they measure it by the steadiness of the person who tucks them in at night. And what my daughters saw was a mother who could schedule every appointment yet still handed her own worth to a man who kept disappearing.

To them I was not the warrior I imagined; I was the doormat they feared becoming.

They couldn't see the storm inside my head: memories half-hidden, a looping soundtrack of questions—*Am I enough? Am I safe? Am I allowed?* They didn't hear the little girl in me still begging for permission to exist.

So while I thought I was showing them resilience, I was teaching them a lesson I never meant to teach:

Love means swallowing yourself to keep the peace.

Endurance is the same as bravery.

A woman can move mountains for her children and still shrink inside her own life.

The realization didn't arrive in a single flash. It leaked in slowly—during therapy sessions, in late-night journal entries, in the silent way Zara's eyes pleaded *Mom, please stand up for yourself* whenever James raised his voice.

The first step toward changing that lesson was admitting it existed at all.

And that, I told myself as I closed my notebook one October night, would be the next question for Thursday:

How do you show your daughters a different kind of strength—one that starts with standing up for yourself?

Chapter 41: Existing Between Heartbeats

There was no grand turning point, no slammed door or miracle phone call that sent me back to Dr. Shivaro's lavender office. I simply... didn't return. Weeks folded into months, then years, and life kept its steady hum: breakfasts to make, shifts to cover, Brielle's medications to sort, light bills to stretch. Hope didn't vanish, but neither did despair; they leveled into something flatter—an almost-silent metronome inside my chest that measured time but never music.

I became exceptionally good at smiling.

At PTA meetings I smiled while mentally tallying which bill might wait another week.

At family cook-outs I smiled while sidestepping questions that skimmed too close to truth.

Even James learned to read that smile—not quite joyful, not quite broken, just... acceptable.

True feelings were swept beneath a rug so worn its threads had fused with the floorboards. Now and then a memory flickered—like an old film reel missing frames:

A girl sitting naked at a dining-room table.

The cries of someone desperate for air.

A little girl twirling in a hooped dress.

Each flash ended before I could study it. Maybe I feared what would surface if I watched the whole reel. Maybe I believed survival required silence. Either way, I chose motion over meaning—laundry, overtime, casseroles for church pot-lucks—anything to outrun the questions I'd never answered.

Existing is deceptively easy: keep breathing, keep moving, keep smiling.

Living—really living—requires room for the echoes to speak.

I hadn't found that room yet.

I didn't even know where to look.

So I measured days in checklist victories: rent paid, meds refilled, homework signed. And inside, a quieter clock kept ticking, waiting for the moment when survival would no longer be enough.

Hours turned into days, days into weeks, weeks into months, and months into years. Zara crossed a college stage in a cap she'd bedazzled herself; Renata shipped out for her first overseas internship; James drifted in and out like weather I'd stopped forecasting. Brielle stayed home with me—my constant sunrise, my constant night-light. Watching my daughters become strong, brilliant women felt like proof I'd done at least one thing right. Their victories were mine, and I tucked them close to my heart like medals no one could take.

And yet—inside—nothing really shifted.

"I think something's broken in me."

One evening, dishes still in the sink, the words burst out of me: "James, I think something is broken inside me."

He stared, confused, while I tried to describe flash-bulb images: a naked girl at a dining-room table, choking sounds in a dark room, a little girl twirling so hard her dress lifted like a bell. I told him the things he'd always done—slamming a cabinet, pouring a drink, laughing too loud—now felt like sparks on dry grass, tiny triggers igniting panic I couldn't tamp down.

"I'm sorry," I said, as if the triggers were my fault. Maybe it was menopause, or empty-nest sadness—anything easier than trauma.

James nodded slowly, suggested I "get it checked," and flipped the TV to sports. He wasn't unkind; he was simply unequipped.

For weeks afterward I drifted in and out of dazes—folding laundry, forgetting which drawer it came from; staring at a blinking cursor, unable to recall the sentence I'd just typed. Fear and anxiety hummed behind every task. My body felt wired for a disaster I couldn't name.

The Night the Locks Gave Way

One still night I lay in bed listening to the house settle—and every locked compartment inside me clicked open at once. Memories didn't trickle; they flooded: voices, smells, rooms I'd nailed shut. Naked terror, ragged choking, dizzy spins beneath a hooped dress and hands clapping too loud.

I gasped so sharply that James jolted awake.

"Nightmare?" he asked.

I nodded—but the past was no longer a rumor; it was a room I was suddenly standing in, walls closing fast.

Reaching for the Girls

The next morning I called Zara first, then Renata.

"I'm going through something I don't understand," I told them.

"What can we do, Mom?" they asked—ready to quit jobs and board planes.

I pictured their bright, unfolding lives and offered the gentlest lie I knew:

"Nothing right now. I'll be okay."

Leaving on My Own Terms

Sleep felt like drowning; waking felt like gasping. One gray Saturday I stood in our bedroom doorway and said, as steadily as I could:

"James, I can't stay here anymore. I'm packing a few things for me and Brielle, and we're leaving."

He didn't believe me at first. We'd been here before. "Don't go," he pleaded. "We can fix whatever you need."

But I felt a certainty I'd never felt: if I stayed, he would leave again—and I could not be left one more time.

I folded two days of clothes into a gym bag, tucked Brielle's blanket under her arm, gathered meds and my notebook. James watched, waiting for me to relent.

"I'm really leaving," I said. "Not this time."

He shook his head, hurt and baffled. "You don't have to do this."

"I do," I answered. "I won't risk being left again."

At the front door he tried once more: "Please stay."

I turned the knob instead, Brielle's hand in mine. "I hope you find what you need," I said.

We stepped into the cool morning air, bags in hand. The door clicked shut behind us—less a slam than a seal—marking not another pause in our cycle, but the end of it ... or so I thought.

Chapter 42: Walking on Shattered Ground

"Her presence shrank the room, but not my spirit. I learned to grow roots even in unfriendly soil."
— Isla Rue

—-

Every decision I made after Brielle and I walked out those doors was born of complete anguish and despair.

I didn't leave with a plan—just a pulse and a promise: never be left again.

But I did have a destination.

A quiet coworker named Donovan handed me the key to an unused country house hidden behind a row of pecan trees. We drove past city limits until gravel crackled beneath our tires. The house was simple clapboard, its paint peeling—but the porch faced open pasture instead of people. No curious eyes. No whispered pity.

Isolation became a reprieve.

Hours turned to days, days to weeks. Brielle painted stones and named constellations.

I opened a notebook and began unlocking the compartments of memory—one door at a time.

The boat: fear in the middle of a still lake, my first taste of betrayal.

The grandmother's kitchen: criticism, the birthplace of self-rejection.

Naming the wounds didn't heal them.

But it showed me where to place the balm.

For the first time, my laughter sounded like it belonged to me.

Donovan listened, no pressure, no expectations, and gently reminded me to stop apologizing for taking up space. Friendship grew into love.

Calm, chaos-free love.

I filed for divorce from James. I closed that chapter.

And for a while, I believed I was finally standing on solid ground.

Then my sister called.

Mom had worn out her welcome under her roof. Could she come to the country house?

I said yes—hope answering for me—and in one week, Mom arrived with boxes and a walker.

Frail body. Same ominous presence.
The hush of the house tightened.
I found myself tuning down my happiness to accommodate her sighs
of "Must be nice."
Donovan noticed.
He asked if I was okay.
I wrote two sentences in my notebook:
Her frailty doesn't erase her power to wound.
I'm allowed to protect my light, even from the people I love.
But old patterns returned like uninvited guests.
Her needs multiplied. She dismissed the joy I tried to share.
I raced to clean accidents, convinced I was slowly destroying
Donovan's serenity.
A nanny-cam revealed her telling a nurse I was cruel. That I had ruined
Donovan's life.
Surprise didn't register.
Only the sting that it still hurt.
I swallowed the truth, told Donovan everything was fine,
and felt healing slide sideways.
I listed my imagined options:
Send her away.
Stay and lose myself again.
Run before being asked to leave.
None of them looked like healing. So I dried my hands.
Opened my notebook.
And wrote:
The next choice must come from the woman I'm becoming,
not the girl who's afraid.
The doors I'd opened were rattling, but they hadn't shut.
I would decide from steady ground,or carve new ground until it felt
steady.

Chapter 43: Back to the Unfinished Page

"She didn't start over. She continued, carrying pieces, rewriting pages, learning the shape of her own voice."

The choice I made came from the girl who was still scared, and unsure how to live her own life. I pointed the car south and let the miles erase what courage I thought I'd earned. By dusk, I was pulling up the rutted drive to James's new place—a single-bedroom fixer-upper with fresh siding on one wall and peeling paint on the rest. A small utility trailer sat in the back.

He met me at the door before I could knock. No "I told you so," no raised eyebrow—just arms wide, steady. I melted into the hug and felt the strange relief of landing in a familiar chapter, even one I'd sworn never to reread.

"Trailer's hooked to power," he said, nodding toward the gravel. "Your mom can have it. I'll help make it livable."

The kindness stripped my defenses. Within an hour, Mom's boxes were stacked in the trailer, Brielle's blanket was on a cot inside the house, and the three of us sat on a half-finished porch while cicadas tuned up.

James spoke first, voice tentative. "I've been working on myself, too." No blame, no shame—only an apology for the hurt he once added to the weight I carried. I hadn't expected him to own anything; the words cracked something open but didn't sting.

We agreed: friendship first. Healthier lines. Help where I needed it.

He still hoped we might become a family again. I didn't know.

For the moment, it was enough just to breathe without judgment.

—-

A Routine of Sorts

Mom in the trailer, TV murmuring game shows.

Brielle and me trimming hedges, folding laundry, reading under the
lone sycamore.
I watched James leave each morning for work, steady and silent—no
need for words.

—-

The Last Message
Donovan's silence was its own ache.
Weeks after I left, a single text arrived:
You will never be free until your mom dies.
Always.
Two sentences—one knife, one farewell.
I stared until the screen dimmed, then tucked the phone face-down.
I whispered an apology he'd never hear and tried not to map the
distance between Always and Never.

—-

What I Carried Forward
I told myself I couldn't ruin another life if I stayed quiet, met needs,
kept my footprint small. But at night, when the house settled and
Mom coughed in the trailer, the notebook on my nightstand
hummed like a live wire:
The next choice must come from the woman I'm becoming, not the
girl who's afraid.
I hadn't made that choice yet—
but the page waited, empty, unfinished,
demanding I pick up the pen again.

Chapter 44: Finding Shore

"The truth doesn't always set you free—but it does loosen the chains enough to let you breathe."

This visit with my father felt like returning to an unfinished page—one I had walked away from, believing the ink had dried. But here he was, the man who shaped my earliest definitions of safety and betrayal, lying frail and fading beneath hospital linens that smelled of antiseptic and lilacs—like the salt-tinged morning air of the ocean, the day everything broke open.

As I entered the room, his eyes lifted to meet mine. "Isla," he said, smiling weakly, "you came."

"Of course I did," I said, taking his hand. "I love you."

His skin was thin as paper, but his grip still carried weight—familiar, heartbreaking. "You know I love you, right?" he asked.

"Yes, Dad. I know." I wiped a tear from his cheek as my own spilled over.

For days, I sat beside him. I fed him, helped the nurses turn him. Sometimes we laughed, and sometimes grief curled around the silence. I waited for the right moment to ask the questions that had shaped so much of my life—and slowly realized: there would be no perfect moment.

So I chose presence over perfection.

"Dad..." My voice cracked. "Did you always know you weren't my real father?"

He closed his eyes. "From the moment I held you," he whispered.

I nodded, the question heavier in the asking than the answer. "What really happened on the boat ride?"

He swallowed hard, as if diving through the memory. "Your mother and I were happy—or so I thought. But things were unraveling. My family warned me: if I fought for you, they'd cut me off. I didn't know how to stand up to them."

I whispered, "So you meant for me not to come back?"

His face crumpled. "I was terrified—of losing everything. I thought, maybe if you weren't there, we could hold the family together."

I remembered the cold that gripped my lungs, the shadows in the water, the seaweed wrapping my ankles. "But I did come back," I said softly.

He squeezed my hand. "And I thank God you did. Isla, I'm so sorry. You were never a mistake. I loved you then. I love you now. Please… can you forgive me?"

A jagged laugh escaped. "I thought you were just trying to teach me to swim."

He chuckled weakly. "Part of me wanted to believe that, too."

We shared that brittle, breaking laugh, two children lost in time, tethered by memory.

I asked, almost to the room itself, "Is that why Grandma hated me?"

He looked away. "She said your mother's life would've been perfect without you."

"And you?" I asked. "Why didn't you come back?"

"I did," he whispered. "I went to your grandmother's, begged for answers. They told me you were living with relatives. That you were in Europe."

I swallowed hard. Europe. The word felt like a punch wrapped in silk—a beautiful lie used to bury years of agony. I wanted to tell him everything: the abuse, the silence, the truth he never saw. But as I looked into his tear-filled eyes, something stopped me. Maybe mercy. Maybe protection. Maybe the part of me that still wanted to believe he would have come for me, if only he'd known.

So I nodded. "Yeah," I said softly. "Europe."

He kissed my forehead. "I thought I'd lost you forever."

I rested my head on his shoulder, listening to the rhythm of his breath, uneven, soft, human.

Outside, the sky turned gold and rose—the colors of endings and beginnings. And for the first time, I didn't feel like I was drowning in the past.

I felt like I was swimming toward shore, with him, at last, beside me.

—-

Chapter 45: The Shore I Walk

Boarding the plane back home, so many thoughts ran through my mind.

It began with the same old mantra: I did ruin a lot of lives.

From the man I thought was my father, I stole his family. My older sister? I stole her father from her. Because of me, he didn't get the time with her he should've had. When he finally could, I was there.

Granted, he loved me. But he had to love me.

I took the life my mother should've had away from her. She could've lived like a queen. But because of me, she didn't.

And my grandmother, Agatha, she truly loved her daughter. She only wanted the best for her. But I was there. I cried silently, staring out the window of that plane.

Every now and then, I touched my skin. And I knew, if I had been born in different skin, maybe the lie I was born into would've been easier to maintain. But the color of my skin betrayed me.

And not once did I put the blame where it belonged.

I didn't ask to be born. I had no control over the things that transpired.

But I carried the blame.

Where do I go from here?

This story doesn't have a fairytale ending.

And I'm sorry if that's what you were hoping for.

You see, healing doesn't come wrapped in beautiful paper tied with a bow. Sometimes, healing comes like the tide—it rushes in, then pulls away. It gives you strength, and in the next moment, it's gone.

But when the tide recedes, you may find a shell. Something beautiful.

Something you can hold onto.

The shell is a piece of yourself that was once lost.

But the ocean is vast. And it may take a lifetime to find all the pieces.

Here I was, walking the shores of my mind.

Filled with conflict. And fury.

Would I allow my past to steal my present?

Do I have an obligation to give up the little moments of peace I've found, to care for someone still capable of tearing through my unsteady shores like a tsunami?

Would I be a caregiver to a soul who had also been hurt, raised in dysfunction deeper than I could imagine?

Can I keep loving someone I know will never love me back?

Could I learn to love, not out of guilt, but because I choose to love freely?

All of these questions ran through me.

Was there enough of me left to be what Brielle needed?

To give my mother what she expected?

And still, find myself?

Because trauma, it continues.

It lingers. It loops.

And dealing with trauma doesn't always look the way movies make it out to.

Sometimes, healing is just not giving up.

Sometimes, healing is loving anyway.

I used to think I was weak. And yes, I made reckless decisions. But I was strong.

I was strong because I didn't let the past change the core of who I was.

Regardless of what had been done to me...

I was love.

And that realization?

That's healing.

Never give up.

"The truth doesn't always set you free, but it does loosen the chains enough to let you breathe."

—-

A few days after returning home, my father passed away.
There was sadness, for a man I hardly knew. And then there was life,
pulling me forward again. I returned to the role I had long known:
caregiver to a mother I had never really had.
I mourned her while she was still alive.
I told myself that in order to survive this life I had chosen, I had to
adopt a certain way of reasoning. I wouldn't allow myself to be hurt
anymore, because the version of her I had needed, the one who
might've loved me the way I longed for, that version had already died.
So I told myself: You are simply caring for a person who needs help.
I could maintain my peace if I kept the two separate, my mother, and
the woman who raised me.
I stopped hoping.
Because when you no longer hope, you are no longer disappointed.
And still, I guard my heart. I suppose I always will.
I have regrets, like most people. But I will never stop learning about
myself.
Healing, I've come to realize, also comes from giving your inner child
permission. Permission to believe they deserved happiness all along.
It's strange, isn't it? That it all came down to permission.
I waited my entire life for someone else to tell me what I could and
couldn't do. For someone to open the door for me. To let me belong.
To let me rest.
And now, here I am, finally giving myself that permission.
Permission to live. Not just exist.
And yet... that has been the hardest voice to listen to.

Acknowledgments

This book would not exist without the love, patience, and resilience of the people who carried me—both in memory and in the present.

To my daughters: Renata, Brielle, Zara, and Renee—thank you for giving me the strength to keep going. You are the light that led me through the darkest of chapters. Your laughter, courage, and love have written themselves into every word of this book.

To my grandchildren—your joy reminded me that healing is not just possible, it is generational.

To my husband, James—your steady presence and belief in me gave me the permission I didn't know I needed. Thank you for holding space when the past felt too heavy.

To Elena—thank you for reminding me that shared memories can still bring warmth, even when they're complicated.

To Dr. Shivaro—your guidance helped me hear the voice I had buried long ago. Your compassion was a lifeline.

To the friends who stayed, even when I was silent—thank you for showing me that love doesn't have to be loud to be real.

And finally, to the quiet girl I used to be—the one who listened, who survived, who hoped... This book is for you.

About the Author

Isla Rue is a memoirist, storyteller, and survivor who writes with raw truth and quiet strength. Through vivid memory and poetic reflection, she explores the resilience of the human spirit in the face of deep trauma and loss.

Born into a world where silence was often survival, Isla now chooses voice — not only for herself, but for others still finding theirs. *What Was Taken, What Remains* is her first memoir: a reclamation of identity, faith, and the girl who kept going.

When she's not writing, Isla finds comfort in stillness, trees, and the kind of conversations that begin with honesty.

www.ingramcontent.com/pod-product-compliance
Lightning Source LLC
Chambersburg PA
CBHW031138130726
47988CB00006B/2431